CARNE

CARNE

MEAT RECIPES FROM THE KITCHEN OF
THE AMERICAN ACADEMY IN ROME

———

BY CHRISTOPHER BEHR

FOREWORD BY TAMAR ADLER

———

PHOTOGRAPHY BY ANNIE SCHLECHTER

ROME
SUSTAINABLE
FOOD
PROJECT

The Little Bookroom

New York

Published by The Little Bookroom
435 Hudson Street, Room 300
New York NY 10014
editorial@littlebookroom.com
www.littlebookroom.com

ISBN 978-1-936941-12-4

10 9 8 7 6 5 4 3 2 1

TABLE OF CONTENTS

12 FOREWORD

14 INTRODUCTION

BEEF & VEAL

21 Rosbeef
Roast Beef

23 Bollito di Manzo
Boiled Beef

25 Piccata di Vitello al Limone
Veal Piccata

28 Scaloppine al Marsala
Veal Marsala

31 Spezzatino di Manzo
Beef Stew

35 Brasato di Manzo
Pot Roast

PORK

40 Porchetta
Roasted Pork with Herbs & Garlic

47 Polenta con Spuntature e Salsicce
Polenta with Pork Spare Ribs & Sausages

50 Maiale "Tonnato"
Pork with "Tuna" Mayonnaise

53 Spalla di Maiale Arrosto
Roasted Pork Shoulder

57 Cotolette alla Milanese
Breaded & Fried Pork Chops

61 Filetto di Maiale in Crosta di Erbe Aromatiche
Pork Tenderloin with Herb & Breadcrumb Crust

63 Maiale al Latte di Mona
Mona's Milk-Braised Pork

LAMB

69 Abbacchio alla Romana
Roasted Baby Lamb, Roman-Style

72 Abbacchio Brodettato
Braised Baby Lamb in Egg, Lemon & Herb Sauce

76 Abbacchio allo Scottadito
Grilled Lamb Chops with Roasted Shoulder

POULTRY

81 Stufato di Pollo con Verdure
Stewed Chicken with Vegetables

83 Pollo alla Romana
Roman-Style Stewed Chicken with Tomatoes & Bell Peppers

87 Saltimbocca di Pollo
Chicken Saltimbocca

89 Pollo alla Diavola
Devil's-Style Chicken

93   Quaglie al Forno
Oven-Roasted Quail

96   Tacchino Ripieno del Giorno del Ringraziamento
Stuffed Turkey for Thanksgiving

RABBIT

103   Coniglio alla Griglia con Salsa di Olive
Grilled Rabbit with Olive Salsa

104   Coniglio alla Cacciatora
Hunter's-Style Rabbit

107   Coniglio Fritto alla Toscana
Tuscan-Style Fried Rabbit

CURED, GROUND & BRINED

113   Prosciutto Cotto
Cooked Ham

117   Pancetta Fresca
Quick-Cured Pork Belly

119   Guanciale
Cured Pork Jowl

121   Polpettone Ripieno
Stuffed Meatloaf

125   Salsiccia di Maiale
Pork Sausage

127   Polpettine di Agnello
Lamb Meatballs

129   Leberwurst
Liverwurst

131   Terrina di Campagna
Country Terrine

134   Conserva di Maiale
Potted Pork

137   Pâté di Fegatini
Poultry Liver Spread

SIDE DISHES

143   Pomodori Verdi Sott'Aceto
Pickled Green Tomatoes

145   Fagioli all'Uccelletto
Beans in the Style of Little Birds

146   Fagioli con le Cotiche
Beans with Pork Skin

148   Cicerchie in Umido
Grass Peas Stewed with Carrot, Celery & Onion

151   Patate al Forno
Roasted Potatoes

152   Insalata di Puntarelle con Acciughe, Pepe Nero e Mozzarella
Puntarelle Salad with Anchovy, Black Pepper & Mozzarella

155   Insalata di Cetrioli Grigliati
Grilled Cucumber Salad

157   Misticanza
       Mixed Foraged Greens

159   Insalata di Radicchio con Mele Verde, Aceto Balsamico e Noci Tostate
       Radicchio Salad with Green Apples, Balsamic Vinegar & Toasted Walnuts

161   Crauti
       Sauerkraut

163   Zucca in Agrodolce
       Sweet and Sour Squash

165   Insalata di Carciofi Crudi
       Raw Artichoke Salad

167   Insalata Tritata
       Chopped Salad

169   Talli di Aglio con Olive e Pomodoro
       Garlic Scapes with Olives & Tomato

BASICS

172   Salse per Bollito
       Sauces for Bollito

172   Salsa Verde
       Green Sauce

172   Salsa Rustica
       Green Sauce with Breadcrumbs & Egg

173   Salsa Rossa
Red Sauce

173   Senape
Mustard

174   Maionese
Mayonnaise

174   Cren
Horseradish Sauce

174   Mostarda di Frutta
Fruit & Mustard Sauce

175   Pearà
Venetian Bread Sauce

176   Polenta

179   Salsa Gravy *or* Il Gravy
Gravy

181   Sale Aromatizzato con Salvia
Sage Salt

181   Spezie per Pâté
Pâté Spices

183   Cleaning Artichokes

185   RECIPE INDEX

FOREWORD

I feel ambivalent and very engaged when I eat meat these days.

I cook most of what I eat, which means I deal directly and intimately with most of the meat I eat. Some evenings I face a fine, golden-skinned chicken, some a lanky rabbit, or fat-capped pink pork roasts. And as I trim fat, remove a chicken neck, pare dark spots from chicken livers, pry the kidneys from a rabbit, I have time to think. And so I do: About *why* I am holding a knife, cleaning and cutting another being for my supper.

The short answer is that I have a taste for chicken, for rabbit, for pork chops, for *crostini toscani*. I have a taste for pork shoulder cooked in milk, for any ragú of any beast on pasta or polenta or risotto.

The longer answer starts with the fact that I've made a few contracts with the world. (It, as far as I can tell, knows nothing of the agreement.) One of them is that I will grapple as directly as I can with the consequences of my human actions, no matter how mixed and muddled they seem. In the case of eating animals, the grappling is straightforward: It entails choosing to *know* rather than to *ignore* the facts of the lives of the animals I eat. It means buying meat from the people who raised it, asking them questions about their ways, not for nostalgic purposes, but because where an animal lived—outside or inside—and what it ate, and where and how it died, all say a lot about whether its life was a good one, a piece of the cosmic puzzle I can get behind, or one I can't.

Even facts like the breed of chicken or cow contain information of moral importance: The older breeds of chickens, neglected by today's industrial farms, had big, strong legs and small breasts, a comfortable anatomical arrangement that made scratching and pecking physically comfortable. Certain breeds of cow and pig gain weight more slowly than others; a cut of meat from one of them will likely be from an animal that had a chance to live a little.

I don't think it's a small matter to take a life, even the life of a well-reared, free-ranging animal. Further answer to the question of why I end up dealing with animals whole, if they are chickens or rabbits, and in large cuts if cows or pigs, is that if I am going to involve myself in the karmic dice roll of eating animals, I feel I only have a leg to stand on if I use every part of them—head to foot, snout to tail, skin to fat to bone. It is faster and easier, of course, to buy meat already cut up. But you can never tell where the rest of the animal landed, and it is often in the trash heap, which is a waste of life. There's nothing morally superior about being reminded before each dinner that one's main dish once pecked or rooted, hopped or hid—that it lived—but it does keep one motivated to save bones for stock, render fat for cooking, turn the last of the roast into a sandwich.

A fortunate fact, at least in America, is that buying whole animals or large cuts—getting the reminders of life, and all of their useful parts—is an inevitable side effect of wanting information: one gets good answers about the realities of animals' lives at farmers' markets, where animals are likely to come feet and beak, head and liver, tail and skin and bone attached, because farmers don't have the time or wherewithal to do all the boning and skinning and transforming into anonymous filets and parts that groceries do.

I would hate to *not* feel ambivalent, as I chop onions and clean anchovies for my *crostini*, peel strips of lemon for my pork in milk. It would make it less likely I would feel as grateful as I do to the animals that gave me the opportunity to serve a meal, to grapple with consequences, to think and be a human with other humans. My ambivalence makes me truly present when I cook meat, and makes me a better cook, each time I decide to not throw out a scrap of fat or bone, thinking of how it once supported a fine, strange living being, as my fat and bones support me. It is a lot to think about. But it seems to me a worthwhile way to spend time.

Tamar Adler
Hudson, New York
May 2016

Tamar Adler is the author of *An Everlasting Meal*. She has cooked at Chez Panisse, is a columnist for the *New York Times Magazine,* and a contributor to *Vogue*.

RSFP AND MEAT INTRODUCTION

Although this is a "meat" cookbook, I can't begin writing about meat without first writing about vegetables. At the American Academy in Rome, the Rome Sustainable Food Project serves mostly vegetables. Every day we make many platters of roasted beets and sweet-and-sour butternut squash, bowls of lemon-dressed oak leaf lettuce and borlotti bean salad, and casseroles of chard gratin. Our lasagna is meatless, as are most of our pasta dishes, and almost all of our soups and risottos. Meat-centric meals are far from the standard at the RSFP.

Meat is scarce in our kitchen and our dining room, and we like it that way for many reasons. The RSFP is tasked with providing healthy, balanced meals to our resident scholars, twice a day, five days a week, and lunch on Saturday, during the Fellows' eleven-month Rome Prize stay. Serving meat as a main course more than two or three times a week is far from sustainable, health-wise or finance-wise.

The meat we buy is a precious, finite commodity. The expectation in many parts of the world for cheap, abundant food, especially meat, has led to factory farming that poisons the earth while mass-producing an overabundance of tasteless, hormone- and antibiotic-laden meat. At the RSFP, we try to set an example of how to be part of a humane and sustainable system. We follow the ideals of socially conscious sourcing and cooking espoused by our founder Alice Waters, the inspirational guiding force behind the RSFP. We buy animals that live a wild, free life on small family farms. Our organic farmers and butchers spend vast amounts of time and energy raising wholesome, healthy animals. We as an institution spend many, many euros to bring in and serve this top-quality product with the reverence and respect it deserves.

Each month during their four-month internship, we take the kitchen interns to visit some of the small family farms and vendors that supply the RSFP. There is no better way to show someone the true value of eating meat sustainably. The interns witness firsthand the time and labor producers put into raising happy animals. For most Americans, meat is something found in the market on a white Styrofoam tray, stamped with a barcode, perfectly shiny and vacuum-packed. By taking the interns to the farms where these animals are raised, they are instilled with a deeper respect for the whole process of eating meat. Practically, in the kitchen, it means they will be more likely to keep their knife sharp for the next meat cutting project, more likely to save that last bit of bone and skin to make a broth or a sauce; they won't waste a single piece of that animal because they have a better sense of where it came from.

At the RSFP, we hark back to the ideals of the *cucina povera*, the traditional cooking of the poor in Italy. We celebrate the entire animal, using all parts of the beast to feed and nourish our community. Nothing is wasted: bones and skin enrich our stocks; organs go into our terrines; trim from all of the butchering projects is ground into sausages and meatballs. The kitchen interns become skilled in dealing with whole animals, which allows them to experience first hand the care with which we treat these animals, even after death.

The meat we serve not only demands thoughtful respect, but celebration! Whereas most of the year we eat meat judiciously, there are times when we all gather as a community to eat grand dinners, often revolving around a large piece of meat. The meat is honored by being the centerpiece of what we hope will be a long-remembered special occasion. We serve a massive Thanksgiving meal to our homesick Fellows every November and hold themed dinners throughout the year that range from corned beef brisket on St. Patrick's Day to the quintessential Italian Ferragosto meal, Roman-style chicken with bell peppers.

At the Academy, in addition to lunch and dinner for the Fellows, we serve a third meal every day. The first lunch, a buffet at 12:15 p.m., is for our *dipendenti*, or workers (the gardeners, maintenance staff, and housekeepers who keep the Academy functioning). Their menu features the simple, balanced, classic flavors of local cuisine, and follows the long-established cadence of the Italian meal: *antipasto*, *primo*, *secondo* with *contorno*, and *dolce*. After my first few weeks at AAR, I realized that I needed to keep my cheffy tricks and techniques well away from the workers' lunch: the Cal-Italian food I had been working on for close to a decade had no place at the lunch table of the *dipendenti*. Arguably, the workers' lunch has taught me the most about *real* Italian cooking, and has allowed us to make it a part of the learning process for our kitchen interns. Anyone can read through the thousands of books that have attempted to package Italian food into neat, easy-to-understand concepts and recipes. But, if you cook for a room full of hungry Romans twenty times a month, you cannot help but acquire a deep understanding of their very specific food beliefs.

I learned this the hard way. Right after I arrived in Rome, I posted a menu for the workers' lunch, which included bucatini with garlic, olive oil, and chili peppers. Shortly after, they approached me. "Are you out of spaghetti?" "No,"

I said, to which they replied, "Then please don't make this with bucatini. Bucatini is for pasta all'amatriciana. You *cannot* make this." I pleaded with them, "Why? Bucatini is very very close to the shape of spaghetti—in my mind it should work out just fine." One of the workers edged in closer, and implored me one more time to put the bucatini away. He explained that I just cannot combine that pasta with that sauce: *NON SI FA*, NOT DONE. It is wrong on a moral level, so wrong that it should not need to be explained! This was the first lesson in understanding how Italians eat. There are rules. The rules can be broken, but only some of the rules, some of the time—and it was not up to me to decide. *NON SI FA*.

The second lunch of the day, a buffet for the Academy's Fellows, begins at 1 p.m. It gives the Fellows a chance to spend an hour or so talking with their peers around a communal table, getting re-energized, and sharing ideas and perspectives before heading back to work in their studios or at their desks. Just like the workers' lunch, the menu for the Fellows' lunch is created by the chef each morning in about 30 minutes. It is based on whatever bits and pieces and leftovers that remain from the previous night's dinner, as well as freshly harvested vegetables and herbs from our backyard organic garden, and the incoming deliveries from our network of farmers and artisanal producers.

This meal has an entirely different structure than the workers' lunch. We serve a soup, a pasta, and four to six *contorni*, or side dishes, as a buffet. A meat-based *secondo* is not served. You may find the occasional anchovy-spiked *puntarelle* salad, or a *pasta alla gricia* anointed with crispy nuggets of salty *guanciale*, or maybe even a smear of rabbit liver pâté on *crostini*, but meat is rarely offered. The buffet is usually almost entirely vegetarian, often accidentally vegan, and laden with whole grains.

Monday through Thursday, our dinner service begins at 8 p.m. Unlike the buffet menu at lunch, this meal is a more structured affair. The tables are draped in white linens, candles are lit, and the food is plated and delivered in three courses by waiters clad in black and white. We serve a meat entree only two or three times a week, and, even then, the meat is often not the star of the show, but the *condimento* for pasta or polenta. Vegetarian, vegan, and gluten-free meals are always available to the community upon request.

My personal favorite is Friday dinner, or Family Night, a buffet that begins at 7 p.m. designed to include the children of the Academy community. Being a New Jersey native, I love to create menus—chicken parm, spaghetti and meatballs, garlic bread, chopped salad, and more—that celebrate Italian-American food.

We try to plan all the dinners a week in advance to accommodate the ordering of proteins, but it doesn't always work out the way we planned, even though we attempt to take into account the unpredictable nature of doing business in Italy. The example

I often make is that I'll call my supplier and order twelve chickens to be delivered on Thursday morning. On Friday afternoon, the truck pulls up and drops off eight rabbits. When I call the vendor to point out the error, the laughing voice on the other side assures me that no mistake was made, that eight rabbits on Friday is pretty much the same as twelve chickens on Thursday, and could I please call back later to complain because it's almost lunch time and this conversation is taking too long. The professional culture shock that I experienced upon moving to Rome will probably keep my blood pressure permanently a few points higher than it should be. But now, after four years in this Roman kitchen, I learned that the same things that drive me nuts about life in Italy, are exactly the same things that make it so endearing.

The mission of the RSFP is not only to be a sustainable model for institutional dining, but also to provide the opportunity for the community of the American Academy to cross-pollinate their ideas. These connections are the driving force behind what we do. We want everyone to understand the relationship between the food that they eat, the life that they live, the art that they make, and the impact they will leave behind. By being careful about our sourcing, conscientious with our cooking, and vocal about our beliefs, we hope our community of interns, scholars, artists, and leaders will carry our message with them wherever they go. That is the understanding we at the RSFP hope to pass on to our diners, and now on to you.

Chris Behr
Rome, May 2016

A practical note about the recipes in this book: In Italian recipes, the equivalent of "to taste" is *quanto basta*, which translates to "as much as is needed" or "enough." It may seem like a small detail, but this concept is specifically representative of the Italian culinary ethos. The English instruction to add a seasoning "to taste" refers to the individual, to the specific cook's subjective definition of what tastes good. *Quanto basta*, however, is a simple instruction: Until it is enough. No more, no less. It implies that there is a universal goal to be reached, and you will know the ideal when you get there.

This is true of all ingredients, but none more important in cooking meat than salt. Most of the recipes in this book include a general guideline for salting meat, but please understand that there is flexibility in those measurements. Don't get bogged down with gram scales and measuring spoons (unless you are curing meat, of course!) and begin to understand how seasoning sausage is different than seasoning a whole chicken. Use repetition and practice to grasp *quanto basta*. The best cooks are those who can really understand when there is "enough": enough salt, enough acid, enough fat, enough spice. Just enough of everything to make a dish harmonious.

BEEF & VEAL

ROSBEEF
ROAST BEEF

Serves 6

Somehow the word rosbeef *has become part of Roman and Italian vocabulary. It is similar to the Dutch word,* rosbief, *but is most likely the result of the Roman propensity to corrupt and squeeze words together into their own vernacular. For example:* Andiamo ragazzi! (Let's go guys!) *becomes* annamo regà! *in the shortened Roman dialect.*

The gentle searing and roasting of the rosbeef, *along with the lengthy rest, results in meat that is rosy and red all the way through, without the gray ring that shows up on many seared-then-roasted beef roasts.*

> 1 (3−4 lb / 1.4−1.8 kg) boneless eye round roast,
>   salted 12 to 24 hours in advance
> Kosher salt
> 2 tbsp vegetable oil, divided

Trim the meat of silverskin and connective tissue. Season generously with salt and allow to rest in the refrigerator for 12 to 24 hours. This will allow the salt to penetrate and begin to tenderize the meat.

When you are ready to cook, use butcher's twine to tie the meat into a uniform roast. This will help to cook it evenly and will provide for more regular slices.

Preheat the oven to 225°F (105°C).

Blot the meat with paper towels to remove any moisture (this will encourage better browning). Use your hands to rub 1 tablespoon of oil all over the meat.

Heat a large skillet. Once it is hot, add the remaining tablespoon of oil to the pan. Add the meat and sear it, maintaining a medium heat as you turn it on all sides to achieve a light golden brown, about 10 minutes. Do not sear the meat too quickly, or the outside of the meat will become tough and stringy.

Once the meat is seared completely, put it on a wire rack set in a roasting pan and put it in the oven. Roast for 1½ to 2 hours, until the meat reaches an internal temperature of 120°F (50°C). Remove the pan from the oven, tent the beef with aluminum foil, and allow it to rest for at least 30 minutes before serving.

BOLLITO DI MANZO
BOILED BEEF

Serves 6

Bollito Misto *is a classic stew, most closely resembling the classic New England boiled dinner or the French* pot-au-feu. *Bollito, in its many regional variations, is eaten throughout northern Italy, and is particularly popular in Emilia-Romagna, Lombardy, and Piedmont. The* Gran Bollito *of Piedmont is all about "sevens": seven cuts of beef* (tagli), *seven supporting cuts* (ammenicoli), *seven condiments (see below), as well as a variety of boiled vegetables. This recipe is my version of the classic* bollito, *which uses just one cut of beef.*

After the meat is removed from its cooking liquid, it is customary to cook vegetables in the broth to serve alongside the meat. The meat is sliced thinly or broken into pieces and served with coarse sea salt and an array of sauces. Any leftover broth can be used as a base for soups and risottos.

The ideal cut of beef for this dish is capello di prete *or "priest's hat." It is a cut that doesn't exist in the U.S., but that is part of the chuck eye roll from the cow's shoulder, known for its abundant fat and connective tissue, two attributes that make it great for braising and stewing. Brisket is a great substitute, or you can use a bone-in piece of meat like shank or short rib.*

The meat itself is not highly flavorful; bollito *is all about the sweet, spicy, and savory sauces that are served with it:* Salsa Verde, Salsa Rustica, Salsa Rossa, Senape, Mostarda di Frutta, Cren, Maionese, *and* Peará, *a Venetian-style bread sauce made with bone marrow, broth, bread, pepper, and Parmigiano Reggiano (see Sauces for Bollito, page 172).*

For best results, the cooked meat should rest in the cooking liquid for 12 to 24 hours before serving. This allows the meat proteins to relax, and the salt and flavorings to distribute evenly throughout the meat and the broth.

> 1 (4 lb / 1.8 kg) chuck eye roast, brisket, bone-in shanks,
>   or short ribs, salted 12 to 24 hours in advance
> Kosher salt
> 3 fresh bay leaves
> 3 cloves
> ½ bottle dry white wine (not oaked)
> 6 large carrots, peeled and sliced

3 large potatoes, peeled and cut into wedges
3 turnips or fennel bulbs, peeled and cut into wedges
Sauces for Bollito (page 172)

Trim the meat of silverskin and connective tissue. Season generously with salt and allow to rest in the refrigerator for 12 to 24 hours. This will allow the salt to penetrate and begin to tenderize the meat.

When you are ready to cook, place the beef in a large pot and add cold water to cover by 2 inches (5 cm). Bring the liquid to a boil, then immediately turn the flame down to a gentle simmer. Use a ladle to skim any scum that rises to the top of the pot (these are coagulated proteins that, if not removed, will make the resulting broth cloudy), then add the bay leaves, cloves, and wine and return to a gentle simmer.

Cook, uncovered, until the meat is fork-tender, but not falling apart. For best results, the meat should be allowed to cool in its cooking liquid overnight. If that is not possible, let the meat rest as long as possible in the liquid before slicing.

Break the meat apart into large chunks, with a knife or two forks. For each diner, place a few pieces of meat in a shallow bowl, ladle the hot broth on top of the meat, and serve with the boiled vegetables and assorted sauces.

PICCATA DI VITELLO AL LIMONE

VEAL PICCATA

Serves 4

The recipes for Veal Piccata and Veal Marsala (page 28) are based on the same technique for cooking scaloppine, thinly sliced pieces of meat that often are pounded into flat, uniform pieces; the saltimbocca method is also similar (page 87). Veal scallops usually come from the leg.

Piccata—from the Italian piccare, meaning to prick, to sting, or to injure with a pike—is a version of scaloppine in which veal scallops are cooked with a sauce of capers, lemon juice, parsley, and butter. The name refers to the sharp flavors of the briny capers and the sour lemon juice. Piccata is an Italian-American invention, probably developed in the 1930s (the traditional Italian dish was most likely scaloppine al limone, with a simple lemon sauce). Piccata is most often made with chicken, not veal, in the U.S.

The common garnish is chopped parsley, but I almost never garnish dishes with raw parsley; I find that it can ruin the first bite with too much "green" flavor. Instead, I add fresh herbs to the pan in the final minutes to briefly cook the herbs and disperse their flavors throughout the dish.

> 1½ lb (680 g) thin veal scallops cut from the leg or shoulder,
>   or butterflied boneless chicken breasts
> Kosher salt
> 4 tbsp vegetable oil
> ½ cup (65 g) flour
> ½ cup (120 ml) white wine (not oaked)
> 2 tbsp salt-packed capers, purged of salt (see below)
> 1 cup (240 ml) chicken broth or water
> ¼ cup (60 ml) lemon juice, plus additional if needed
> 12 sprigs parsley, picked and roughly chopped
> Coarsely ground black pepper
> 2 tbsp butter, cubed and chilled

Place the veal or chicken pieces on a cutting board, cover with a layer of plastic, and gently pound the meat using the flat side of a meat mallet to achieve very thin, even slices. Sprinkle each piece, on both sides, with salt. (Be careful not to use too much salt, as the pieces of meat are very thin. The meat does not need to be salted ahead of time—although I suggest doing so in most of the other meat recipes in this book—because the scallops are thin and they already have been tenderized by pounding. I do not add black pepper at this stage; the pepper can burn when sautéed, and I do not want to accentuate the pepper flavor.)

Purge the capers by rinsing off the excess salt, then simmer them in water for about 2 minutes. (Do not boil.) Drain, add fresh water, and simmer the capers for another 2 minutes. Drain and set aside.

In a large, shallow pan, heat the oil over a medium flame until hot but not smoking.

While you're waiting for the pan to get hot, dredge each scallop in flour. (Note: I almost never season flour. If salt, pepper, or other spices are added to the flour, it is impossible to control how much will get into each portion. You can potentially under- or over-season the meat. It is much better to season each piece individually, and then dredge it in flour.)

Shake off excess flour from each piece. (After the meat is coated with flour, it is important not to let too much time pass before cooking. If the meat hydrates the flour coating, it will be impossible to brown the scallops evenly.)

After the *scaloppine* have been floured, immediately cook them, in batches, in the hot pan. Do not overcrowd the pan. Add additional oil as necessary.

Each scallop should be cooked for approximately 2 minutes on each side without moving. Resist the temptation to move the pieces; it is important that the meat is cooked quickly while also browning. Make sure to control the heat of the pan as you cook; do not let the bottom of the pan burn. Remove the "just barely cooked" *scaloppine* to a plate to rest. It is ok if there are a few undercooked or raw spots because the meat will finish cooking in the sauce.

Once all the meat is cooked and resting, pour out any excess oil from the pan. Pour in the wine, and, still over medium heat, gently scrape up any brown bits from the bottom of the pan. When the smell of alcohol has subsided, add the capers, the broth or water, and the lemon juice, and bring to a boil. As the sauce is gently reducing, add the chopped parsley, a few twists of black pepper, and the cold, cubed butter. Simmer the sauce for a few minutes until thick and glossy, then return all of the *scaloppine* to the pan. Coat them with the sauce, adding more broth or water as necessary to achieve the right consistency. (If you did not shake off enough flour after dredging the *scaloppine*, the excess flour may make the sauce too thick.) Work quickly, as the thin slices of meat can very easily overcook and become tough. Taste and adjust the sauce with salt and lemon juice if needed.

Plate the *scaloppine*, pouring over any extra sauce from the pan.

SCALOPPINE AL MARSALA
VEAL MARSALA

Serves 4

Marsala is a variation of scaloppine that may have been created in the 19th century by English families living in western Sicily, where Marsala wine is produced. Another theory is that the dish is of Italian Jewish origin. Like Picatta, chicken, rather than veal, is more popular in the U.S.

> 1½ lb (680 g) thin veal scallops cut from the leg or shoulder, or
>   butterflied boneless chicken breasts
> Kosher salt
> 4 tbsp vegetable oil
> ½ cup (65 g) flour
> 2 shallots, minced
> ½ lb (225 g) button mushrooms, washed, dried, and thinly sliced
> ⅓ oz (10 g) dried porcini mushrooms, rinsed and soaked in hot water
> 1 cup (240 ml) Marsala wine
> 1½ cups (360 ml) chicken broth or water
> 12 sprigs parsley, picked and roughly chopped
> Coarsely ground black pepper
> 2 tbsp butter, cubed and chilled

Place the veal or chicken pieces on a cutting board, cover with a layer of plastic, and gently pound the meat using the flat side of a meat mallet to achieve very thin, even slices. Sprinkle each piece, on both sides, with salt. (Be careful not to use too much salt, as the pieces of meat are very thin. The meat does not need to be salted ahead of time—although I suggest doing so in most of the other meat recipes in this book—because the scallops are thin and they already have been tenderized by pounding. I do not add black pepper at this stage because the pepper can burn when sautéed, and I do not want to accentuate the pepper flavor.)

In a large, shallow pan, heat the oil over a medium flame until hot but not smoking.

While you're waiting for the pan to get hot, dredge each scallop in flour. (Note: I almost never season flour. If salt, pepper, or other spices are added to the flour, it is impossible to control how much will get onto each portion. You can potentially under- or over- season the meat. It is much better to season each piece individually, and then dredge in flour.)

Shake off excess flour from each piece. (After the meat is coated with flour, it is important not to let too much time pass before cooking. If the meat hydrates the flour coating, it will be impossible to brown the scallops evenly.)

After the *scaloppine* have been floured, immediately cook them, in batches, in the hot pan. Do not overcrowd the pan. Add additional oil as necessary.

Each scallop should be cooked for approximately 2 minutes on each side without moving. Resist the temptation to move the pieces; it is important that the meat is cooked quickly while also browning. Make sure to control the heat of the pan as you cook; do not let the bottom of the pan burn. Remove the "just barely cooked" cutlets to a plate to rest. It is ok if there are a few undercooked or raw spots because the meat will finish cooking in the sauce.

Once all of the meat is cooked and resting, add the shallots to the remaining oil in the pan and gently cook until softened and translucent. Add the sliced button mushrooms to the pan and sauté until cooked through.

Lift the rehydrated porcini mushrooms out of their liquid. (Do not pour them through a strainer because it will agitate the sediment and dirt that has sunk to the bottom.) Pour the soaking liquid through a coffee filter and reserve. Chop the porcini and add them to the pan.

Pour the Marsala into the pan to deglaze, scraping up any brown bits. Simmer until the Marsala has reduced to a syrupy consistency, then add the chicken broth or water and the porcini liquid. As the sauce is gently reducing, add the chopped parsley, a few twists of black pepper, and the cold, cubed butter. Simmer the sauce for a few minutes until thick and glossy, then return all of the *scaloppine* to the pan. Coat them with the sauce, using more water or broth as necessary to achieve the right consistency. (If you did not shake off all the excess flour after dredging the scallops, the sauce may be too thick.) Work quickly, as the thin slices of meat can very easily overcook and become tough. Taste and adjust the sauce with salt and more liquid if needed.

Plate the *scaloppine*, pouring over any extra sauce from the pan.

SPEZZATINO DI MANZO

BEEF STEW

Serves 6 to 8

Spezzatino *comes from the Italian verb* spezzare, *which means "to break," and refers to the meat that is "broken," or cut into small pieces.* Spezzatino *can be made with all kinds of meat, including pork, beef, or lamb.*

For this dish, never buy packaged meat that is labeled "stew meat." Often the pieces of meat are cut into different sizes and can be from different parts of the animal, which makes it difficult to cook the pieces evenly; some pieces will still be tough at the end of cooking, while some will be falling apart. It is better to ask the butcher for meat from a single muscle group. The best cut for this dish is beef chuck or shoulder, specifically a chuck roll or chuck eye roast.

Like most stewed or braised dishes, spezzatino *tastes much better after sitting overnight in the cooking liquid. This allows the meat proteins to relax, and the salt and flavorings to be evenly distributed throughout the meat and the broth.*

If you can afford the time to let the dish rest overnight, it is best not to add the vegetables or herbs until reheating the meat and sauce the next day. Large or starchy vegetables, such as potatoes, should be blanched first before adding to the reheating meat, in order to avoid overcooking the meat.

The recipe can be adjusted to fit the season or the weather. In springtime, the meat can be lightly seared, cooked with white wine, and might include peas, carrots, fava beans, asparagus, and soft herbs such as parsley. In summer, the meat also would be lightly seared, cooked with white wine and extra broth, and might include cherry tomatoes, zucchini, and basil. In fall, the meat would be more heavily seared, cooked with rosé or red wine, and the dish might include mushrooms or squash, and sage, and be served over barley. In the heaviest winter version, the meat can be floured to make a thicker sauce, heavily seared, cooked with red wine, perhaps with pancetta, include root vegetables and hard herbs like rosemary or sage, and be served with a grain, such as farro.

Below is a version I often make in spring.

1 (4 lb / 1.8 kg) beef chuck roast, prepared and salted 12 to 24 hours in advance
Kosher salt
3 tbsp vegetable oil
3 carrots, peeled and cut into large chunks
2 celery stalks, peeled and cut into large chunks

1 large onion, peeled and cut into large chunks
2 fresh bay leaves
2 tbsp chopped hard herbs (sage, marjoram, rosemary in any combination)
2 tbsp tomato paste
2 cups (480 ml) white wine
3 cups (720 ml) beef broth, chicken broth, or water
6 carrots, peeled and cut on the bias into 2-inch (5-cm) pieces, blanched until
    75% cooked
12 whole red potatoes, scrubbed, halved if large, and blanched until
    75% cooked
2 cups (280 g) shelled English peas (frozen are OK)
2 tbsp chopped parsley
Coarsely ground black pepper

Trim the meat of silverskin and connective tissue. Cut into 1½-inch (4-cm) pieces, season with salt, and allow to rest in the refrigerator for 12 to 24 hours.

When you are ready to cook, prepare the *soffritto*. Put three carrots, the celery, and the onion in a food processor and chop to a very fine, watery paste. Reserve.

In a Dutch oven or large, heavy pot with a lid, heat the oil until very hot but not smoking. Blot the meat with paper towels to remove any moisture (this will encourage better browning). Sear the meat cubes in batches until browned on all sides, about 10 minutes. It is important to cook the meat in many batches to avoid overcrowding in the pan. The meat needs to sear, not to steam. Remove all the meat to a platter and let rest while you begin the sauce.

Add the minced vegetables to the pan that the meat was browned in. Add more oil if necessary. Cook the *soffritto* until it is softened and translucent. Add the bay leaves, the hard herbs, and tomato paste. Cook the tomato paste until it has turned deep brick-red.

Deglaze the pan with the wine, scraping up the browned tomato-y bits from the bottom of the pan. Once the smell of alcohol has subsided, return the meat to the pan along with any accumulated juices.

Add the broth or water and bring to a boil. The meat should be almost, but not entirely, submerged. Turn down to a simmer and use a ladle to remove any scum or grease that floats to the top.

Cook, uncovered, until the meat is tender but not falling apart, then add in the large pieces of blanched carrots and potatoes. When those vegetables are almost done, fold in the peas and chopped parsley. Adjust the consistency of the sauce with broth or water, check the seasoning, and serve.

BRASATO DI MANZO
POT ROAST

Serves 6 to 8

This is one of the dishes that we like to feature at Friday family night dinners at the Academy—it's classic American comfort food. I like to serve it with wide, eggy pappardelle, which mimics the classic American pot-roast-and-egg-noodle pairing. It's also great served with creamy mashed potatoes or polenta.

Like most stewed or braised dishes, brasato tastes much better after sitting overnight in the cooking liquid. Ideally, the meat should rest in the sauce for 12 to 24 hours before slicing it and serving.

> 1 (4 lb / 1.8 kg) chuck eye roast or chuck roll, prepared and
>   seasoned 12 to 24 hours in advance
> Kosher salt
> 2 tbsp vegetable oil
> 2 large onions, peeled and sliced
> 4 carrots, peeled and sliced into ½-inch (1-cm) pieces
> 2 celery stalks, sliced into ½-inch (1-cm) pieces
> 2 fresh bay leaves
> 2 garlic cloves, peeled and smashed with the side of a knife
> 2 tbsp tomato paste
> 2 tbsp hard herbs, such as rosemary and thyme, chopped
> 1 cup (240 ml) red wine or dark beer
> ½ cup (120 ml) sweet vermouth
> 4 cups (960 ml) beef or chicken broth or water
> 1–2 tbsp red wine vinegar
> Coarsely ground black pepper

Trim the meat of silverskin and connective tissue, tie into two small roasts, season with salt, and allow to rest in the refrigerator for 12 to 24 hours.

When you are ready to cook, heat the vegetable oil in a large pan until hot but not smoking. Blot the meat with paper towels to remove any moisture (this will encourage better browning). Brown the meat evenly on all sides, about 15 minutes. Make sure to regulate the heat so that the pan does not burn.

Once the meat has browned, remove it to a plate to rest while you make the braise.

Keep the pan on a medium flame and add the onion, carrot, celery, bay leaf, and garlic. If the pan is too dry, add some additional oil. Once the vegetables are softened, add the tomato paste and hard herbs and fry until the tomato turns a brick-red color. Deglaze with the wine or beer and the vermouth, scraping up any browned bits from the bottom of the pan. Once the smell of alcohol has subsided, add the seared roasts back to the pan and pour in the broth.

Bring the liquid to a boil, and then turn down to a simmer. Skim any scum or grease that floats to the top with a ladle. Simmer, uncovered, until the meat is fork-tender but not falling apart.

Remove the meat to a plate to cool while you finish the sauce. Discard the bay leaves. Pass the vegetable braise through a food mill or puree it in a food processor to make a thick sauce. Adjust the consistency of the sauce with broth or water if it is too thick. If it is too thin, put it back on the heat and simmer until it is the consistency of gravy. To counter all the meat and vegetable sweetness, finish the sauce with a capful or two of red wine vinegar. (The vinegar adds that slightly sour addictive quality that keeps you coming back for more.) Salt and pepper to taste.

Remove the strings from the meat and slice into ¾-inch (2-cm) slices. Pour the hot gravy over the meat and serve.

PORK

PORCHETTA

ROASTED PORK WITH HERBS & GARLIC

Serves 12 to 15, with leftovers

I learned how to make this from my mentors, Nate Appleman and Liza Shaw, when I was a young apprentice cook at A16 restaurant in San Francisco. It was one of the first dishes I was entrusted to execute on my own; of course, I messed up royally. Later, when I was the chef de cuisine at SPQR, another San Francisco restaurant, porchetta sandwiches were one of the most popular items on the menu. I now serve them for the outdoor picnic at the Academy during Trustees Week.

Many regions in Italy have some version of porchetta, with the key difference being how the whole, deboned pig is seasoned before roasting. In Rome, the pork is heavily salted, and garlic, rosemary, and black pepper are added. In Umbria, the porchetta is prepared with lard, garlic, black pepper, wild fennel or fennel pollen, chopped entrails, and salumi bits. In Treviso, the mixture includes black pepper, wild fennel, garlic, and white wine. In Sardinia, porchetta—called porceddu in the local dialect—is roasted over myrtle and juniper wood. The best porchetta I ever had was just over the Lazio border in Abruzzo; it had herby, salty pockets that literally left my mouth watering.

I like to combine the more austere Roman porchetta seasonings—usually just garlic, sage and/or rosemary, and black pepper—with the more interesting Umbrian version, in which a paste made of lard and other salumi bits or entrails is mixed with herbs and fennel pollen, and spread on the inside of the cavity.

True porchetta is always a whole or a half of a roasted, deboned pig, served at room temperature. Since eating a whole (or even a half!) of a pig is far beyond most people's needs, here I give instructions for a more home-friendly version.

My porchetta begins with a fresh, trimmed pork belly. I use an X-Acto knife or razor to make crosshatches on the skin side. I find the smaller the squares of skin, the better chance the meat has to achieve the ideal crispness. I like to season HEAVILY with both the fine salt and grainy salt. The fine kosher salt penetrates deeply into the meat (kosher salt has a specific crystal shape that facilitates that), and the large grainy sea salt will not melt entirely, ensuring crunchy, salty pockets within the meat.

You have two options for the meat filling: you can wrap the prepared belly around a cleaned and seasoned pork loin OR around several long pieces of cleaned pork shoulder. There are pros and cons for both. The loin is lean, so it cooks faster and yields meatier slices with less squidgy, fatty bits; the downside is that it can easily be overcooked. The shoulder is much fattier, with more connective tissue, so it needs to be cooked long and at a low temperature to break down; its downside is that when the porchetta is carved, the shoulder does not result in the perfect, meaty circles that the loin provides.

The most important detail, no matter which pig piece you use, is the marinating time before cooking. The pork pieces need to sit—salted, seasoned, and tied—for several days. This will allow flavor to penetrate deep into the meat and also make the pork more tender. Also, the long marinating time permits the proteins to denature, and then coagulate when cooked, which melds the meat layers, so you get nice, sliceable portions. For the best crispy skin, the skin should be dry, but not overly dry like a piece of leather.

> 1 (6 lb / 2.7 kg) pork belly, skin-on
> 1 (3 lb / 1.4 kg) pork loin roast or pork shoulder, prepared
>   and seasoned 24 to 48 hours in advance
> ¾ cup (225 g) kosher salt
> ¼ cup (75 g) coarse grain sea salt
>
> Marinade:
> 8 garlic cloves, peeled and smashed into a paste with the
>   side of a knife
> Zest of 4 lemons, grated on a microplane
> 12 sprigs rosemary, picked and roughly chopped
> 6 sprigs sage or thyme leaves, picked and chopped
> 2 tbsp fennel seeds, lightly toasted and roughly chopped
> 1 tbsp coarsely ground black pepper
> 1 cup (240 ml) rendered lard or bacon fat, softened [can
>   substitute olive oil, but only use ½ cup (120 ml)]

Place the pork belly on a large cutting board. Use an X-Acto knife or razor to make crosshatches on the skin side at ½-inch (1-cm) intervals. Cut all the way through the skin. Flip the belly over (meat side up) and score it a few times lengthwise with a chef's knife. These cuts will help the meat form an even roll.

If using pork loin for the filling of the porchetta, make sure the roast is totally clean of all bones and cartilage. Trim the fat cap so it is a just a small layer (¼-inch / .5-cm or less). If the loin piece is longer than the pork belly, trim the ends off so it fits

neatly along the length of the belly. If the belly is too long, trim away any excess from either side.

If using pork shoulder, halve the shoulder into two long pieces, then clean away any excess fat, veins, glands, and thick pieces of connective tissue. Lay the shoulder pieces end-to-end along the length of the pork belly. If you have any scrap pieces of belly or shoulder, you can lay them inside as well.

Season all the pork pieces with salt, pressing the salt into all parts of the meat, the skin, and all the nooks and crannies. Allow the salt to absorb while you assemble the rub.

Combine all the marinade ingredients and mix well. The lard should be pliable and easily spreadable. Mix the lard and herb paste all over the inside (meat side) of the pork belly, as well as the pork pieces that will become the "filling."

With the long side of the pork belly facing you, wrap the belly tightly around the pork filling. Tuck the loin or shoulder pieces back in if they start to squeeze out. Use butcher's twine to tie the log very tightly at 2-inch (5-cm) intervals.

Allow the seasoned *porchetta* log to rest in the refrigerator like this, uncovered, for at least 24 and up to 48 hours. This step will help dry the skin, ensuring crispiness, and allow all the meat pieces to better stick together.

Remove the pork log from the refrigerator at least 2 hours before you plan to cook it, so it can come to room temperature. Place the *porchetta* on a rack in a deep-rimmed roasting tray. Roast in a preheated 275°F (135°C) oven for 3 to 4 hours. If using pork shoulder, the internal temperature of the meat needs to be above 180°F (80°C) for at least an hour to ensure tender meat. For me, the best way to determine if the pork is done is to use the meat thermometer not to take the temperature, but, rather, as a probe. Insert it into the middle of the roast. It should slide in and out of the center with little to no resistance. If using pork loin, it will be done closer to the 3-hour mark, with an internal temperature goal of about 150°F (65°C).

Once the "no resistance" test is passed for the shoulder, or you hit about 150°F (65°C) with the loin, take the pork out of the oven and decant all the roasting juices and fat (save for making roasted potatoes!). Raise the heat to 450°F (230°C), and put the pork back in the oven to crisp the skin. Watch the pork carefully as the skin begins to crisp up; it should take anywhere from 15 to 25 minutes for the pork skin to bubble up and get very, very crunchy. At this stage and high temperature, the pork can burn easily; so do not leave the *porchetta* unattended.

Remove the *porchetta* from the oven and allow to rest uncovered for 45 minutes to an hour so the internal juices have a chance to settle and redistribute. Serve in thick slices at room temperature.

POLENTA CON SPUNTATURE E SALSICCE
POLENTA WITH PORK SPARE RIBS & SAUSAGES

Serves 6 to 8

This is a dish of pork ribs and pork sausages stewed with tomato and served over polenta. In the Italian way of thinking, the meat and sauce are condiments for the polenta; the meat is not the main event, the polenta is.

This dish is a typical cold-weather dish served in Lazio. Originally, it was a celebratory meal served on the day or the day after a pig was butchered. It is now part of most Roman trattoria menus during the winter.

At home, this dish is often served on a large piece of wood or large cutting board instead of a platter, truly "family-style," with everyone diving in to the communal pile of food. It is also a recipe typical of the cucina povera, in which all parts of the animal are used and celebrated, and the meat is only a garnish for the more stomach-filling and affordable polenta.

Although most Italians would never do it, I peel the silverskin off the bottom side of the ribs. The membrane does not break down when cooked, so by peeling it off you expose the tender meat underneath. Also—maybe more important—it doesn't get stuck in your teeth when you really go to town on the ribs!

I prefer spare ribs to baby back ribs, but both will work. Furthermore, I prefer not to use St. Louis–style spare ribs, in which the sternum, cartilage, and rib tips are removed; I prefer the whole sparerib in all its glory. The chewy cartilaginous bits on the end of the rib are fun to gnaw on and give more depth to the sauce.

I suggest using canned, peeled, whole San Marzano–style tomatoes. I never buy chopped canned tomatoes—there is no guarantee that they are not just scraps and stems and bits left over from the canning process. I prefer to see the whole tomatoes, and crush them myself. My favorite way is to pour them out into a bowl and crush them by hand, resulting in different-sized bits of tomato. For dishes like this, I prefer not to use a food mill or food processor to puree the tomatoes, because the texture of the resulting sauce is too uniform and not rustic enough. Also, it's fun to get your hands dirty!

Freshly milled, high-quality polenta is an ingredient that is just as important as fancy olive oil. Do not skimp on quality here. This dish is most often served with yellow cornmeal, but white or even buckwheat polenta (taragna) works well too.

12 pork spare ribs
2 tbsp kosher salt, plus additional for seasoning
2 tbsp olive oil

6 pork sausages (homemade, page 125, or bought)
2 cloves garlic, peeled and smashed
1 carrot, peeled and minced
1 celery stalk, minced
2 onions, peeled and minced
1 pinch chili pepper flakes
2 sprigs rosemary, picked and roughly chopped
2 fresh bay leaves
1 cup (240 ml) dry white wine
3 (28 oz / 794 g) cans whole San Marzano—style tomatoes, crushed by hand
½ cup (58 g) grated pecorino Romano (or Parmigiano)
1 recipe Polenta (page 176)

Trim the spare ribs of silverskin and separate them into single bones. Rub the ribs with 2 tablespoons of salt and allow to rest in the refrigerator for 6 to 8 hours, or overnight. (Unlike other large pieces of meat, ribs do not need as much time to rest after being salted because they are mostly bone.)

Heat a large Dutch oven or high-sided skillet over a medium flame. When the pan is hot, add the olive oil. Wait a few seconds; when the oil shimmers, add the pork ribs and begin to brown on all sides. Cook in two batches if necessary; if you crowd the pan, the ribs will boil, not fry, and they won't brown the way they should. When all the ribs are seared, remove them to a plate and leave all the fat in the pan.

Sear the sausages on all sides, not to cook them through—they will finish in the sauce—but to impart a roasted "brown" flavor to the meat and the sauce. Make sure to control the heat. If the heat is too high, the sausage casings will split or the bottom of the pan will burn and foul the rest of the sauce. Remove the browned sausages to the plate with the ribs.

Tip off any excess fat from the pan, leaving behind about 3 or 4 tablespoons. Add the garlic, carrot, celery, and onions and sweat over medium-low heat until the vegetables are soft and the onions are translucent.

Add in the chili pepper, rosemary, and bay leaves and stir to combine. When you can smell the aromatic chili and herbs, deglaze the bottom of the pan with the wine, scraping up any brown bits. Cook the *soffritto* until the smell of alcohol subsides (the mixture will still smell like wine, but not like alcohol).

Add the crushed tomatoes and stir to combine. Add the pork ribs to the pot and bring to a gentle simmer. Don't be afraid to add water to the pot in small increments to keep the ribs just barely submerged. Start making the polenta by putting the water on to boil.

Cook the ribs in the sauce for about an hour, until the meat is tender but not falling away from the bone, stirring occasionally to make sure the ribs are cooking evenly and not sticking to the bottom of the pot.

If the pot is large enough, add the seared sausages and cook an additional 15 to 20 minutes, until the sausages are cooked through and the ribs are totally tender. (If the pot is not big enough to fit the ribs and sausages together, simply remove the ribs to a plate while the sausages cook in the sauce, then add the ribs back into the sauce a few minutes before serving in order to reheat them.)

Use a ladle or spoon to remove any excess orange grease that bubbles to the top as the pork cooks. Don't take it all out though—it's really delicious. Taste the sauce and adjust for salt if necessary. Keep in mind you will be finishing this dish with salty pecorino, so don't overdo the salt.

To serve, lay down a generous blanket of polenta on the biggest serving tray you have. Spoon the ribs, sausages, and rich *sugo* over the polenta. Dust heavily with pecorino, roll up your sleeves, and enjoy.

MAIALE "TONNATO"
PORK WITH "TUNA" MAYONNAISE

Serves 6

This is the RSFP version of the classic Vitello Tonnato. It's a dish served at room temperature, so it's good during the hot summer months. We like to use lean pork loin or tenderloin as a substitute for the veal, and we leave out the tuna, which is generally not a sustainable fish; that's why it is not really tonnato. Instead, to get that umami-packed fishiness, I use anchovies and a few drops of colatura, the Italian fish sauce descended from the garum of ancient Romans. I also blend in a few cooked egg yolks to provide the extra-thick creaminess that the canned tuna would provide.

When buying pork, especially tenderloin, it is important to make sure that the meat is not "enhanced," that is, injected with a brine of sodium, preservatives, and flavorings, a common practice in the U.S.

> 1 (4 lb / 1.8 kg) center-cut boneless pork loin roast or 2 (2 lb / .9 kg)
>   pork tenderloins, prepared and salted 12 to 24 hours in advance
> ¼ cup (75 g) plus ¼ tsp kosher salt, plus additional if needed
> ¼ cup (60 ml) vegetable oil
> 3 egg yolks, room temperature + 2 whole eggs, hard-boiled
> 2½ cups (600 ml) any neutral vegetable oil, divided
> ½ tsp coarsely ground black pepper
> 4 tablespoons lemon juice
> 1 tsp colatura
> 4 whole salt-packed anchovies, purged of salt, cleaned, and deboned
> ½ cup (75 g) salt-packed capers, purged of salt (see below)
> ½ cup (95 g) cornichons or 1 medium pickle, chopped roughly
> Coarsely ground black pepper
> 2 bunches of arugula or watercress, washed and dried

Trim the meat of silverskin and connective tissue and tie with butcher's twine into neat roasts. Season with salt and allow to rest in the refrigerator for at least 12 and up to 24 hours.

Purge the capers by rinsing off the excess salt, then simmer them in water for about 2 minutes. (Do not boil.) Drain, add fresh water, and simmer the capers for another 2 minutes. Drain and set aside.

When you are ready to cook, preheat the oven to 375°F (190°C). Blot the pork dry with paper towels. Drying the pork will ensure a better, more even sear. Heat a large, thick-bottomed sauté pan over a medium flame. When the pan is hot, add the oil. When the oil is hot but not smoking, begin to sear the pork on all sides. (Control the heat to make sure the meat is getting a nice, even sear. If the meat is seared too hard or browns too much, the texture of the finished meat will be tough and stringy.) The pork is done when it is light golden brown.

Place the pork on a wire rack set in a roasting pan, and roast until the meat reaches an internal temperature of 135°F (60°C), 1 to 1½ hours. Use a meat thermometer to check the thickest part of the meat.

Remove the pork to a plate and allow to rest until it comes to room temperature. While the meat rests, make the sauce.

In a large bowl, whisk together the three egg yolks with ¼ teaspoon salt and a few drops of water until pale yellow. Starting with a drop at a time, then a slow, thin stream, drizzle in 2 cups (480 ml) of the vegetable oil while whisking continuously.

Whisk in 3 of the 4 tablespoons of lemon juice, the pepper, and the *colatura*.

In a blender, or with a handheld immersion blender, mix the remaining ½ cup (120 ml) oil, the anchovies, the hard-boiled egg yolks, the pickles, and half of the capers into a rough paste. Add the paste to the mayonnaise. If needed, adjust the mayonnaise with the remaining tablespoon of lemon juice, as well as with additional salt and pepper. The sauce should be quite strong and tangy. For best results, allow the mayonnaise to rest for several hours for the flavors to develop.

With a sharp knife, slice the pork as thinly as possible, and shingle on plates. Generously spoon the sauce over the meat. Garnish with a few twists of black pepper, the remaining capers, and a few leaves of arugula or watercress.

SPALLA DI MAIALE ARROSTO

ROASTED PORK SHOULDER

Serves 6 to 8

This is a go-to dish for the RSFP kitchen: simply roasted pork. When most people think of pork roast, they imagine pork loin. A delicious cut, yes, but it is extremely lean and can very easily be overcooked. At the Academy, I prefer to roast pork shoulder. Unlike the loin, the meat is full of intramuscular fat and connective tissue. After a long, low, slow roast, the connective tissue breaks down to become gelatinous, giving that unctuous, rich mouthfeel for which pork is so famous.

Because of the simplicity of this preparation, the quality of the pork can really shine. We use a rare breed of pig called Cinta Senese (Belt of Siena), which refers to the sash of white hair that encircles the black pigs. The breed was almost wiped out during WWII and was also endangered by the widespread industrialization of meat processing in the late '70s and '80s, but is now making a comeback due to a few dedicated breeders in Tuscany. I use this pork not only because the meat is first-rate, but also because I want to support the network of super-small producers who are the backbone of the RSFP food sourcing. The vendor I use for this pork is called Lo Spicchio.

The flavor of the meat is a result of free-roaming grazing by the pigs, in wooded areas, feeding on grasses, roots, tubers, and acorns. The meat is a deep red. Although this breed is not available in the U.S., any other kind of full-flavored heritage pork can be used— just make sure to stay away from supermarket "enhanced" pork that is pumped full of water, salt, and flavorings.

In the U.S., the cut that works best for this recipe is called pork shoulder or pork butt. It is full of fat and collagen-rich connective tissue, which makes it perfect for this cooking method.

The technique I use here is called "broasting," a combination of braising and roasting. The meat is roasted in an open pan in the oven, while partially submerged in a flavorful liquid. As the meat is turned several times during cooking, it is glazed by the simmering fat and jus, which impart a roasted flavor to the sauce.

For this recipe, I make a simple broth with the reserved pork bones and water only. Making a proper French stock with lots of aromatics is unnecessary in this case; the broth is infused with flavor as the meat cooks, and doubling up on the vegetable flavor will only hide the taste of the beautiful pork.

Our favorite way to serve this pork is over a bed of stewed cicerchie, *a legume that is grown in the home region of the RSFP's most beloved farmer, Giovanni Bernabei. This legume is unusual in that it contains a very powerful neurotoxin. The peas must be soaked overnight and then blanched three times before cooking (page 148). After blanching, I like to stew down the grass peas with vegetables, and then, right before serving, fold in a puree of all the remaining sauce, vegetables, herbs, fat, and drippings from the roasted pork.*

> *1 (4−5 lb / 1.8−2.3 kg) pork shoulder roast, bones removed and*
> *reserved, prepared and salted 18 to 24 hours in advance*
> *½ cup (150 g) kosher salt*
> *6 sprigs rosemary, leaves picked and minced*
> *1 tsp coarsely ground black pepper*
> *1 tsp ground fennel seed*
> *3 cloves garlic, peeled and smashed with the side of a knife into a paste*
> *4 tbsp olive oil, divided*
> *1 fennel bulb, sliced into 6 or 8 wedges*
> *2 red onions, peeled and quartered*
> *2 carrots, peeled and cut in half*
> *1 tbsp tomato paste*
> *2 fresh bay leaves*
> *½ bottle inexpensive dry white wine or rosé*
> *Pork broth, as needed*
> *Apple cider vinegar to taste, optional*
> *1 recipe Cierchie in Umido (page 148)*

Use a sharp paring knife, score a 1-inch (2.5-cm) crosshatch pattern into the fat on the top of the roast (there may be a fat cap depending on the type of roast; skip this step if no fat is present on the outside of the meat). Be careful not to slice into the meat. Rub the meat on all sides with the salt.

In a small bowl, mix together the rosemary, pepper, fennel seed, garlic, and 2 tablespoons of oil. Rub the mixture all over the pork, making sure to get into the crevices that you scored into the fat. Place the roast in a large baking pan, cover with plastic, and allow to rest in the refrigerator for 18 to 24 hours to allow the salt to penetrate and tenderize the meat.

While the meat is resting, make the pork broth. Preheat the oven to 400°F (205°C). Take the reserved bones and put them in a roasting pan. Roast for 30 to 40 minutes until they are a deep golden brown. Remove the bones to a large stockpot, top off with water, and simmer for 6 to 8 hours, skimming any scum or grease that floats to the top. If the liquid reduces too much, add more water to ensure the bones stay submerged. Strain the broth through a fine strainer, discard the bones, and reserve the liquid. You should have about 3 quarts.

Remove the pork from the refrigerator at least 2 hours before you intend to cook it. Using butcher's twine, tie the meat into a long, even roast. If the pork roast is really big, you can cut it in half lengthwise to make two, smaller roasts.

Preheat the oven to 325°F (165°C). Place a large Dutch oven or high-sided thick-bottomed pan on the stovetop over a medium-high flame. When the pan is hot, add the remaining 2 tablespoons of oil and wait a few seconds until it shimmers. Add the large chunks of fennel, onion, and carrot. Let the vegetables sit, without stirring, until they become golden brown on one side, then continue turning them until they have browned on all sides, about 15 minutes.

Stir in the tomato paste and bay leaves and cook until the tomato turns a brick-red color. Deglaze the pan with the wine, scraping up any browned bits from the bottom, and boil until the smell of alcohol has subsided.

Place the roast(s) in the pan and add pork broth until it comes halfway up the side of the meat. Return to a boil on the stovetop and then place in the oven. Broast the pork for 3 to 4 hours, flipping the meat over every 30 minutes, until a small paring knife can be inserted in the thickest part of the meat with only a small amount of resistance. (You want the pork to be tender, but still able to be sliced neatly. If you overcook it, all is not lost—the meat will begin to fall apart in large shreds, not unlike Carolina-style pulled pork. If the pan dries out while cooking, top it off with pork broth to keep the meat halfway submerged during the entire cooking process.)

When the meat is done and nicely glazed, remove the pan from the oven and allow it to cool to room temperature on the countertop, turning the meat a few times as it cools. Ideally, let the meat rest in its own sauce, overnight, in the refrigerator. This will dramatically improve the flavor and texture of the meat.

When you are ready to eat, remove the meat from its sauce, cut away and discard all the strings. Strain the braising liquid, reserving the cooked vegetables. Allow the liquid to separate, and remove most, but not all, of the rendered fat. Reserve the extra fat for the *cicerchie* side dish—don't throw it away!

Remove the bay leaves and discard them. Using a food mill with the small plate (preferred) or food processor, puree the cooked vegetables. Mix the puree and the reserved braising liquid in a saucepan to make a thickened, tasty sauce. Bring the sauce to a simmer and check for seasoning. If the sauce tastes a bit flat or too vegetable-sweet, add a capful of vinegar to balance the sauce (I like apple cider vinegar). The sourness will give the sauce an "addictive" quality. You may use all of the vegetable puree or pork broth for the sauce, but if there is any tasty liquid left, reserve it to add to the *cicerchie*.

Slice the pork into ¼-inch (.5-cm) slices, and shingle in the same pan used to roast the pork. Cover liberally with the sauce and bake in a 325°F (165°C) oven, just until reheated, about 10 minutes.

Serve the warmed pork over a bed of stewed *cicerchie*, garnished with the remaining sauce from the pan.

COTOLETTE ALLA MILANESE
BREADED & FRIED PORK CHOPS

Serves 4

This is a dish that I like to serve in the summer, just above room temperature, with a cherry tomato, cucumber, and wild arugula salad that is piled on top of the fried cutlets right before they're sent out to the dining room. The acidic juices from the tomatoes dress the pork like a sauce, and help cut through the fattiness of the dish. Despite being fried, if these cutlets are cooked correctly, they will absorb very little oil.

Cotoletta *comes from* costoletta *or "little rib," indicating that the pounded, breaded cutlet still has the rib attached. Traditionally,* Cotoletta alla milanese *is a breaded and deep-fried veal cutlet served simply with a wedge of lemon. Small chops from milk-fed baby lamb, prepared in a similar style, are very popular in Roman trattorie. What chicken fried steak is to the U.S., what Wiener Schnitzel is to Germany, what* milanesa *is to Latin America and* tonkatsu *is to Japan,* Cotolette alla milanese *is to Italy.*

Many cuts of pork can be used in this dish. My favorite is a bone-in, blade-end pork chop or rib chop that comes from the part of the loin closest to the shoulder; it is full of marbled fat and connective tissue. When properly tenderized and trimmed, these chops are more interesting to eat and have better texture than the center-cut pork loin chops, which can dry out easily when cooked. For a boneless, super-tender result, use pounded medallions of pork tenderloin.

Noteworthy variations on alla milanese *are* alla parmigiana *(made with tomato sauce and either mozzarella or burrata);* alla palermitana *(a Sicilian version made without flour or egg, brushed with oil, dipped in seasoned breadcrumbs, and pan-fried with lemon leaves, for their perfume);* alla orecchia d'elefante *or elephant's ear (prepared with a cutlet that is butterflied and pounded so very thin that it's often bigger than the plate it is served on). Italian restaurants prefer this last preparation for its quick cooking time.*

> 4 (6–8 oz / 170–227 g) bone-in, blade-end pork loin chops,
>   prepared and seasoned 2 to 6 hours in advance
> 1 tbsp kosher salt, plus additional if needed
> ¾ cup (96 g) all-purpose flour
> 3 large eggs
> 2 tbsp milk or water
> 2 cups (480 ml) vegetable oil for frying
> 2 bunches wild arugula, washed, and dried
> 1 pint ripe cherry tomatoes, halved if small, quartered if large

1 cucumber, peeled, seeded, and diced into ½-inch (1-cm) cubes
Juice of half a lemon
1 tbsp olive oil

Clean the pork chops of any excess fat and silverskin, especially from the top (outer) part of the pork loin. (Be sure to cut off all the fat. Once the chops are breaded, the fat underneath will not render and is not enjoyable to eat.)

Since these shoulder chops can be tough, tenderizing them is very important. Take one chop, pat it dry with a paper towel, and put it inside a zip-lock bag. Do not seal the bag, but lay it flat on the cutting board. With the flat side of a mallet, hit the meat with steady and even force, starting at the center of the meat and using the mallet to push outwards toward the edge of the meat. If you hit the meat too hard, it may tear. Be careful not to hit the bone or you may put a hole in the bag. Continue to pound the meat until it is about ¼-inch (.5-cm) thick, then remove to a plate.

Once all four chops are pounded, season them evenly on both sides (don't forget the rib) with the salt. Mound all the chops on a plate, cover with plastic, and refrigerate for 2 to 6 hours. Because the cutlets are so thin, I do not recommend salting them overnight; to salt them that long can cause the meat to take on a "cured" chewy texture.

When you are ready to cook, set up a breading station. Line up three deep serving plates, each one large enough to hold a single cutlet. In the first, place the flour, shaking the plate back and forth to make an even layer. Next, whisk the eggs and milk or water together with a fork until homogenous and pour the mixture into the second plate. Finally, pour the breadcrumbs into the third plate, again shaking back and forth to make an even layer. (I do not season the egg, the flour, or the bread-crumbs. I find that salting the cutlets when they are raw, as well as salting them after they are fried, is enough. By salting the cutlets directly, I can see exactly how much salt is going where; when adding salt to big amounts of flour or breadcrumbs, it's hard to control the even distribution of the seasoning.)

Working one at time, and using one hand for dry ingredients and the other hand for the egg, start to bread the cutlets. Dip the first cutlet in the flour, flipping it over several times to ensure complete and even coating. Shake off all excess flour with a few flicks of the wrist, then dip the meat into the egg wash. Again, make sure it is fully coated and then allow the excess egg to drip off back into the bowl. (It is important to let the extra egg drip off; allow at least 30 seconds to a minute of "drip-time" per cutlet. Too much egg left on the cutlet can result in an unpleasant eggy crust under the fried breadcrumb layer.) Now dip the cutlet into the bread-crumbs, turning it over several times and using your hand to press the crumbs into the meat, making sure that all of the cutlet and the rib are well coated. Shake off excess breadcrumbs. (If you do not shake off the excess breadcrumbs, you can foul the frying oil very quickly, which results in off-tasting cutlets.)

Complete this process for the remaining pork chops, and once they are breaded, allow them to rest on a wire grid on the countertop for about 30 minutes. (This drying time will help the flour to hydrate and the breadcrumbs to dry and to better adhere to the pork.)

Pour the vegetable oil into the frying pan and turn the flame to low. The oil should not fill the pan more than ¼ of the way up the side. If it does, change to a bigger pan or do not use all of the oil. Use the thermometer to keep an eye on the oil as it slowly heats to 360°F (180°C).

Once the oil is hot, fry one or two cutlets at a time, without overlapping them, about 4 minutes on each side. Remember to let the oil recover its temperature in between fry sessions. Remove the fried cutlets to a wire rack on a tray lined with paper towels, and while they are still warm, season each one with a small pinch of salt. (It is important to season immediately after frying; the bubbling oil will help adhere the seasoning to the breading.) If frying one at a time, place the cutlets on the grid, and keep them warm in a low oven while you work.

Mix together all the remaining ingredients and mound the salad on top of each cutlet. Serve right away.

FILETTO DI MAIALE
IN CROSTA DI ERBE AROMATICHE

PORK TENDERLOIN WITH HERB & BREADCRUMB CRUST

Serves 4

This dish was designed by my trusty sous chef, Domenico Cortese, for the annual Cortile Dinner during Trustees Week at the Academy, when all of the benefactors come to Rome. It is probably the most important and fun meal of the year in the RSFP kitchen.

This is an ideal dish for a warm-weather banquet, as it can be prepared in advance, has a quick cooking time, and is delicious served just above room temperature. It's great paired with the Grilled Cucumber Salad (page 155).

> 2 (1 lb / 454 g) pork tenderloins, seasoned at least 12 hours in advance
> 2 tbsp plus a pinch of kosher salt, plus additional if needed
> 1 lb (454 g) boneless, skinless chicken breast, diced and chilled
> ½ cup (120 ml) heavy cream, chilled, plus additional if needed
> 2 tbsp parsley, finely chopped
> 1 tsp fresh mint, chopped
> 1 tsp fresh chives, chopped
> 1 sprig rosemary, picked and chopped
> ½ sprig thyme, picked and chopped
> ½ tsp coarsely ground black pepper
> 3 cloves garlic, peeled and minced
> Olive oil

Season the tenderloins with the salt at least 12 hours before cooking, and refrigerate.

When you are ready to cook, using a food processor, puree the chilled chicken breast with the cold cream and the pinch of salt until the mix is totally smooth. You may need a little more cream or water to get the mixture to puree properly.

Smear the puree on all sides of the pork so the meat is completely covered in a thin layer. The mixture is sticky; you may want to wear gloves or wet your hands.

Mix all the herbs, the pepper, and the garlic into the breadcrumbs.

Roll the coated pork in the seasoned breadcrumbs and return the meat to the refrigerator for at least 30 minutes and up to 2 hours to set the crust.

Preheat the oven to 400°F (205°C). If you have a convection fan, turn it on.

Once the meat has rested and set, place the pork on a wire rack in a roasting pan and drizzle with olive oil. (The oil helps to brown the breadcrumbs.)

Roast for about 15 to 20 minutes, until a probe thermometer inserted in the fattest part of the loin registers about 135°F (60°C). The meat should still be pink. Allow the meat to rest for 5 to 10 minutes and slice on the bias to serve.

MAIALE AL LATTE DI MONA

MONA'S MILK-BRAISED PORK

Serves 4 to 6

At the Academy, this dish is legendary. It was introduced by the RSFP founding chef, Mona Talbott, who passed on the recipe to her successor, Chris Boswell; he, in turn, passed it on to me.

The dish originated in Northern Italy—Bologna and Emilia-Romagna—but can be found all over Italy. Traditionally, the recipe calls for a boneless pork loin, but that muscle is not suited to a long braise in liquid, so I use pork shoulder to ensure an unctuous, juicy result. The lactic acid in the milk helps to tenderize the meat. The cooked-down sauce resembles ricotta, with delicious caramelized curds.

As with many Italian recipes, there are many versions. The nineteenth-century Italian food writer Pellegrino Artusi suggests using pork and milk only; more modern recipes call for a wide range of aromatics, including herbs, lemon, and spices.

A thick-bottomed pot is necessary for this dish. Do not use a non-stick vessel because the milk curds will not caramelize.

Since the dish is very rich, Mona suggests serving the pork with simple boiled vegetables such as cabbage, turnips, carrots, fennel, or beans, or topped with a mixture of fried sage, lemon zest, and chopped parsley.

> *1 (4–5 lb / 1.8–2.3 kg) bone-in pork shoulder roast,*
> *seasoned 12 to 24 hours in advance*
> *¼ cup (75 g) kosher salt, plus additional if needed*
> *Coarsely ground black pepper, plus 1 additional tsp*
> *2 tbsp butter*
> *2 tbsp olive oil*
> *3 sprigs rosemary*
> *3 small sprigs sage*
> *6 cloves garlic, peeled*
> *2 lemons, zested in large strips with a vegetable peeler*
> *2 quarts (1.9 liters) whole milk*

About 12 to 24 hours before cooking, season the pork roast with the salt and pepper and if you prefer a tidy roast, tie the meat with butcher's twine to maintain the shape.

When you are ready to cook, preheat the oven to 325°F (165°C). In a large, thick-bottomed, high-sided pot that can fit the pork roast, add the butter and olive oil and warm over medium heat. After the butter has foamed and subsided (the foam is the extra water boiling away from the butter; this step is necessary in order to guarantee the milk solids in the butter will brown evenly), add the roast to the pot and brown evenly over medium heat on all sides, about 10 minutes. Be careful to control the heat and make sure the bottom of the pan does not scorch. Take the pork out of the pot and set it aside while you make the *soffritto*.

Tip off any excess fat from the pan, leaving behind about 3 tablespoons. In the fat, over medium-low heat, sizzle the rosemary, sage, additional teaspoon of pepper, garlic, and lemon zest. Do not brown the aromatics, just soften them.

When the *soffritto* is fragrant and softened, put the pork roast back in the pan and pour in the milk. The milk should just barely cover the roast (depending on the size of the pot). Cover the pan and put it in the oven. Turn the meat several times as it cooks and add more milk or water if necessary to keep the meat partially submerged in liquid. The pork is done when the meat offers little to no resistance when pierced with a fork—about 2½ to 3 hours. The meat should be tender, but not falling apart.

Remove the pork roast to a plate to rest while you finish the sauce. The milk sauce should have thickened and have tiny brown caramelized curds. If it hasn't, reduce the sauce on the top of the stove until it is the consistency of gravy. Taste for seasoning and adjust.

To serve, pull the meat apart into big chunks and spoon the creamy sauce, with the zest and the herbs, over the meat. Serve immediately.

ABBACCHIO ALLA ROMANA
ROASTED BABY LAMB, ROMAN STYLE

Serves 4

This is the quintessential Roman meat dish, best during the spring months when lamb is in season. It is always part of the Easter meal.

Abbacchio *is the Roman word for baby lamb, a bastardization of the verb* abbattere, *to butcher, which Romans turned into* abbacchiare. *As I mention elsewhere, Romans love to create their own words. The lambs are 20 to 30 days old when butchered and weigh between 10 and 20 pounds (4.5–9 kg). They have never been fed anything other than their mothers' milk, which is why the meat is so pristine, light-colored, and tender.*

In the RSFP kitchen, we break down the entire lamb and roast all the parts. We set aside all of the organs for coratella, *a specifically Roman dish of stewed lamb innards, often served with onions or artichokes. The dish below is inspired by the recipe in Oretta Zanini de Vita's* The Food of Rome and Lazio, *which we give to all the RSFP interns when they arrive.*

For me, the most amazing part of this dish is that all parts of the abbacchio *can be cooked together, at the same time. The meat is so young and tender that the parts of the lamb that usually take longer to cook—the shanks, shoulder, and neck—take the same amount of time as the "quick-cooking" parts, such as the loin. Most lamb in U.S. supermarkets is between 6 and 12 months old, often imported from Australia or New Zealand, but ideally this dish is made with local lamb, which is in season only in the spring in the U.S. Finding this type and variety of meat in the U.S. can be difficult or impossible for anyone who doesn't have a close relationship with a local farmer, so I have suggested easy-to-find alternatives that will offer great results.*

Romans do not eat lamb that is cooked medium or medium-rare, as is customary in the United States. Most Romans are very skittish about eating seemingly undercooked food. The beauty of this dish is that all of the meat is cooked until it is well done, but remains juicy and tender.

If you are cooking an older piece of lamb, it is important to remove the fell, the thin, papery membrane on the outer layer of fat on the lamb. Younger animals have not developed this yet. The fell should be removed because it can add a very gamey flavor and will hinder the salt and seasoning from being absorbed by the meat.

In this recipe, the meat is salted before the aromatic marinade is applied. This is a small detail, but very important. I do not put the salt in the marinade mix because you cannot guarantee that it will be evenly applied to all parts of the meat. Also, the oil will prevent the meat from absorbing the salt. Another important detail is that the vinegar is added a short time before cooking—just long enough for it to tenderize the meat. If the meat marinates too long in the vinegar, the acid "overcooks" the meat and makes it mushy.

Of all the meat dishes in the book, this is the one that really shines with the Oven-Roasted Potatoes (page 151). The potatoes are cooked alongside the lamb, absorbing all the aromatic juices of the wine, broth, herbs, and meat.

> *4 (8–12 oz / 227–340 g) lamb shoulder chops, cut about 1-inch (2.5-cm) thick or 2 whole racks of lamb ribs, cut into 2 or 3 bone pieces, or a combination of both cuts, seasoned and marinated 8 to 12 hours in advance*
> *2 tbsp kosher salt, plus additional for seasoning*
> *1 tsp coarsely ground black pepper, plus additional for seasoning*
> *2 tbsp olive oil*
> *2 cloves garlic, peeled, smashed, and chopped finely*
> *3 sprigs rosemary, picked and chopped finely*
> *6 leaves sage, chopped finely*
> *4 sprigs thyme, picked and chopped finely*
> *2 salt-packed anchovies, cleaned, purged of salt, mashed into a paste*
> *1½ tbsp white wine vinegar, plus additional if needed*
> *1 cup (240 ml) dry white wine*
> *Lamb broth (made from any extra bones) or chicken broth or water*
> *1 recipe Oven-Roasted Potatoes (page 151), optional*

8 to 12 hours before you plan to cook the lamb, coat the pieces with the salt and pepper. Place the pieces in a large bowl while you prepare the marinade.

In a small bowl, mix the oil, chopped garlic, herbs, and anchovy paste until combined. Using your hands, apply the marinade to the seasoned meat. Make sure all surfaces of the meat are coated. Place the meat in a large plastic bag or large roasting pan covered with plastic and refrigerate for 8 to 12 hours. If using a plastic bag, handle gently so the bones do not puncture the plastic.

When you are ready to cook, preheat the oven to 350°F (175°C).

If you are making the Oven-Roasted Potatoes, blanch them and set aside.

Remove the marinated lamb from the refrigerator, and place it in a large roasting pan along with any accumulated juices and extra marinade. While the oven is preheating, add the vinegar to the marinade in the pan and with your hands, once again rub the marinade over the lamb, making sure the vinegar is evenly distributed and the lamb is evenly coated.

If using, add the warm, blanched potatoes to the roasting pan.

Roast the lamb for approximately 1 hour and 10 minutes. About every 20 minutes, quickly pull the tray from the oven (you do not want the oven or the lamb to cool down) and sprinkle with about ¼ cup (60 ml) of the wine and about ¼ cup (60 ml) of the broth or water. After about 30 minutes, turn the pieces of lamb and potatoes over with a spatula. The lamb is done when it is golden brown, tender, and pulls easily away from the bone. Adding the wine and broth during cooking helps to glaze the pieces of meat nicely.

Remove the lamb (and potatoes) to a serving platter to rest while you make the pan sauce. Pour off all the pan juices into a clear container and wait 3 or 4 minutes for the fat to separate. Skim off the fat and discard. Place the degreased pan juices in a small saucepan and keep warm on the stove with a low flame. Put the roasting pan onto the stovetop over a medium flame. When the pan is hot again (sizzling, but not hot enough to burn the brown bits stuck to the bottom of the pan), pour into the pan about ½ cup (120 ml) of any remaining broth, or water. Scrape up all the tasty brown *fond* from the bottom of the pan and pour the sauce into a small saucepan. Taste for seasoning, adding more water if it's too salty or thick, and a small amount of vinegar if it tastes a bit flat. Pour the sauce over the meat and potatoes and serve immediately. You can strain the pan sauce for a more refined presentation, but this is a rustic dish, and I really like the caramelized bits and pieces from the pan in my sauce.

ABBACCHIO BRODETTATO
BRAISED BABY LAMB IN EGG, LEMON & HERB SAUCE

Serves 4

Brodettato *means "in a little broth." This is a classic Roman springtime dish, especially at Easter, the lamb and egg being symbols for crucifixion and resurrection.*

In the kitchen, we call this "lamb carbonara" because of its eggy, peppery sauce.

The technique used is similar to the French method of making a liaison, *in which eggs and cream, with a little lemon juice, are added to a sauce for thickening power and fatty mouthfeel. The most important step is tempering, in which small amounts of hot broth are slowly whisked into the eggs to prevent them from curdling when added to the pot. Raising the temperature of the eggs before adding them ensures that the mixture will not scramble and provides for a thick, creamy sauce.*

The classic version of this dish calls for marjoram, and maybe a little parsley, but I also like to add mint and chives so the green, fresh flavor of the herbs really cuts though the eggy sauce. Mint is a natural partner for lamb, and the high note from the chives works well with the egg and lemon sauce.

The herbs can be prepared and picked in advance, but they should not be chopped until the last moment before going into the sauce. Herbs are aromatics, and cutting them too far in advance can diminish the perfume of the herb or lead to murky, compost-y flavors.

This recipe can be made with boneless lamb stew meat from the shoulder or leg, but bones add to the flavor of the dish. Bone-in lamb shoulder chops or lamb shanks, or a combination of the two, work well. Lamb necks are also a perfect and inexpensive cut to use. You can ask at your deli counter or butcher for prosciutto fat.

> 4 bone-in lamb shoulder chops, about ¾-inch (2-cm) thick, or 4
> small lamb shanks, seasoned 12 to 24 hours in advance, bones
> reserved for broth, optional
> 1½ tbsp kosher salt, plus additional for seasoning
> ½ cup (64 g) all-purpose flour
> 3 tbsp olive oil
> ½ cup (125 g) prosciutto fat or pancetta, minced
> 1 garlic clove, peeled and smashed
> 2 large spring onions, white and light green parts only, or 1 white
> onion, peeled and finely chopped

1 cup (240 ml) dry white wine
3 sprigs marjoram, picked, stems reserved
Lamb broth (made from any extra bones), chicken broth, or water
4 large egg yolks
8 sprigs parsley, picked
2 sprigs mint, picked
12 chives
½ tsp coarsely ground black pepper
Juice of 1 large lemon

Make sure the meat is trimmed of all excess fat and silverskin. Season the meat with 1½ tablespoons of salt and allow to rest in the refrigerator for 12 to 24 hours.

When you are ready to cook, remove the meat from the refrigerator and dab off any excess moisture with a paper towel. In a large bowl, toss the meat with the flour, making sure to coat all sides. Be very careful to knock off all excess flour as you remove each piece of lamb from the bowl. Too much flour can result in a starchy, gluey sauce.

In a large pan (with a lid) that can fit all of the lamb pieces, begin to sear the lamb. Heat the pan over a medium flame, and when the pan is hot, add the olive oil and swirl to coat the bottom. Sear the lamb pieces gently until they are golden brown on all sides. (If all of the lamb cannot fit in the same pan, sear the lamb in batches to avoid overcrowding.) Maintain the heat so neither the meat nor the flour gets too dark; burnt flour has a very bitter taste.

Once all the lamb has been browned, begin the *soffritto*. (If the pan has scorched or looks dark, begin the *soffritto* in a clean pan.) Over medium-low heat, slowly render the prosciutto fat or pancetta. When most of the fat is rendered and the pieces are fully translucent, add the garlic and onion. Slowly sweat the vegetables until they are soft and sweet.

When the vegetables are softened, deglaze the pan with white wine. Be sure to scrape up any brown bits from the bottom of the pan. Once the wine has reduced and the smell of alcohol has subsided, return the lamb to the pan, along with the marjoram stems. Heat the lamb or chicken broth or water and add it to the pan until the lamb is almost submerged.

Braise the lamb, partially covered with a lid to let some moisture escape. Add more broth or water as necessary to keep the meat partially submerged. The shoulder chops can take as little as 30 minutes, whereas the shanks can take 90 minutes or more. When the meat is tender but not falling away from the bone, turn the heat off, remove the marjoram stems from the braise, and allow the meat to rest in its liquid and cool slightly.

Begin the egg sauce: In a small bowl, whisk the egg yolks together. While continuously whisking, slowly ladle a few ounces of the warm lamb liquid into the eggs until the eggs are as warm as the lamb.

Bring the lamb back to a very low simmer, pour in all of the tempered egg mixture, and stir to combine.

Continue to gently stir the pot as the egg sauce begins to thicken, about 6 minutes. Be careful to maintain a low heat so the eggs do not catch to the bottom of the pan and scramble.

Finish the sauce by roughly chopping the herbs and adding them to the pot. Add the pepper and lemon juice. The acid from the lemon juice and the green from the herbs should be balanced by the fatty lamb and eggy sauce. Adjust as necessary to get a pleasing balance of flavor. Taste and adjust for salt. The sauce should be thick enough to cling to the meat—the consistency of carbonara pasta sauce—but no thicker. Add warm broth to thin the sauce if necessary. Serve immediately.

ABBACCHIO ALLO SCOTTADITO
GRILLED LAMB CHOPS WITH ROASTED SHOULDER

——————

Serves 4 to 6

This is another Eastertime dish from Lazio, seen on menus year-round, although it is best in April through June during spring lamb season. Abbacchio allo scottadito *is marinated and quickly grilled lamb chops. The bones are still hot when you eat them; thus* scottadito, *which means "burn the fingers." The word is often bastardized on Roman trattoria menus, written as* abbacchio ascottadito, *following the Roman penchant to smash words and phrases together.*

Because here at the Academy we use only two to three lambs per dinner, to feed about fifty people, it's impossible to serve every diner a large enough portion of chops only. To supplement the chops, we bone out the legs and shoulders of the lambs and tie them into small, seasoned roasts so that each diner gets a slice or two of tender lamb roast, in addition to the chops.

We always use whole animals here, but for the home cook I have specified more common retail cuts. It is important to seek out young, tender lamb. Older, gamier lamb, especially the shoulder and leg, does not work as well for this recipe. If older lamb is used, increase the cooking time significantly, for both the chops and the roast.

> 2 racks of lamb, trimmed, cut into single chops (bones not
>   Frenched) and 2 boned-out lamb shoulders or legs from
>   a young lamb, seasoned and marinated 12 to 24 hours in
>   advance
> 3 tbsp kosher salt
> 2 sprigs rosemary, picked and finely chopped
> 6 sprigs thyme, picked and finely chopped
> 2 garlic cloves, peeled and made into a paste
> 2 tsp fennel seeds, roughly chopped or pounded in a mortar
> 1 tsp coarsely ground black pepper
> ½ cup (120 ml) olive oil, plus additional for searing
> Lemon wedges

Trim the meat of excess fat and connective tissue and rub it with 3 tablespoons of salt. Prepare the marinade by mixing together the rosemary, thyme, garlic, fennel seeds, pepper, and olive oil. Smear the marinade on the chops and the boned shoulders or legs. Return the seasoned chops to the refrigerator while you finish the roasts.

Using butcher's twine, tie the seasoned shoulders or legs into small roasts and allow them to rest in the refrigerator, along with the chops, for 12 to 24 hours.

When you are ready to cook, preheat the oven to 350°F (175°C).

Place the roasts in a roasting pan and place it in the oven. Depending on their size and the age of the lamb, they will take about an hour. You can tell when they are done if a sharp paring knife can be inserted and removed with no resistance. Remove the roasts from the oven and let rest on a plate. When cool enough to handle, remove the strings.

While the roasts are resting, cook the chops. Over a high flame, add a small amount of oil to lightly coat the bottom of a large cast-iron pan, and heat it until very hot. Cook the chops as fast and as hard as possible. Ideally the thin chops will still be a nice, pink color after a very quick sear in the pan. [If you do not have a large enough pan to cook the chops without crowding, use an outdoor grill or a very hot 500°F (260°C) oven.]

While the chops are briefly resting, slice the roast into thin slices. Serve both immediately with any accumulated juices, along with lemon wedges.

POULTRY

STUFATO DI POLLO CON VERDURE
STEWED CHICKEN WITH VEGETABLES

———

Serves 4 to 6

This is an interpretation of classic chicken soup, a comfort dish served at the Academy in the fall, as colder weather sets in, when the Fellows are feeling a bit of homesickness after their first three months in Rome. This is also a variation on bollito; the vegetables are cooked in the flavorful broth that results from first poaching or simmering pieces of meat.

1 (4 lb / 1.8 kg) whole chicken, back removed and reserved, legs separated
    from breast, seasoned at least 6 hours in advance
2 tablespoons plus 2 pinches kosher salt, plus additional for seasoning
2 carrots, peeled and cut on the bias into 2-inch (5-cm) chunks
2 parsnips, peeled and cut on the bias into 2-inch (5-cm) chunks
2 small leeks, white and light green part only, left whole
4 small white turnips, peeled and cut in half, greens reserved and chopped
6 small red potatoes, cut in half if larger than a golf ball
1 3-inch (7.5-cm) piece of Grana Padano rind
1 small bunch parsley, picked, stems reserved
Olive oil
Coarsely ground black pepper

Season the chicken pieces with salt and let them rest in the refrigerator for at least 6 hours and up to overnight.

When you are ready to cook, fill a large pan halfway with water (about 4 quarts), and bring it to a simmer on the stovetop. Season the water with two pinches of salt. (I add this small amount of salt to the water to prevent osmosis from drawing salt out of the seasoned chicken meat.)

When the water is just about to simmer, carefully drop in the chicken legs and cook at a very low and steady simmer until the meat is tender and just beginning to fall away from the bone, about 30 to 40 minutes. Remove the legs from the pot and let them cool on a plate while you poach the breasts.

Cook the breasts in the same broth for 15 to 20 minutes. Use the tip of a paring knife to check the thickest part of the chicken breast, nearest to the bone. The meat should be opaque throughout, and no longer translucent. Remove the breasts to the plate with the legs and allow them to cool slightly. Keep the chicken broth at a simmer.

While the chicken is cooling, cook the vegetables in the broth. Start with the carrots and parsnips together, followed by the leeks (boiled whole in order to keep their shape) and turnips together, and finally the potatoes. Simmer each group of vegetables gently until easily pierced with the tip of a paring knife. The vegetables should be fully cooked but not mushy or falling apart. As each vegetable comes out of the liquid, reserve to a platter and sprinkle with salt. Cut the leeks in half lengthwise once they have cooled.

When all of the vegetables are cooked, add the Grana rind, the cleaned chicken back, and parsley stems to the pot and slowly reduce the liquid by about half. Skim any foam that rises to the top as the pot simmers.

Clean the chicken; remove the skin and discard. Pull the meat away from the bones carefully, trying to keep the chicken in the largest possible pieces. Make sure to clean away any bones, veins, or cartilage, especially the rubbery tendons at the end of the leg muscles. Taste the meat for salt and adjust if necessary.

Once the broth is reduced and flavorful, remove the parsley stems, chicken back, and cheese rind. You should have about 6 cups (1.4 liters) of liquid. Add in the chopped turnip greens and simmer for a few moments.

Assemble the dish by carefully adding the vegetables to the simmering broth. Finely chop the parsley leaves and add to the broth. Finally, add in the picked chicken meat. Stir to incorporate, being careful not to break up the pieces of meat. Check the liquid for seasoning and add salt if necessary. If too salty, add a little water.

Use a large spoon or ladle to plate the stew. The meat and vegetables should be served with a small pool of broth on the plate. Finish the dish with a drizzle of olive oil and a generous grinding of black pepper.

POLLO ALLA ROMANA

ROMAN-STYLE STEWED CHICKEN WITH TOMATOES & BELL PEPPERS

Serves 4

This is the quintessential Ferragosto dish, served in Rome during the hours-long Sunday lunch on the weekend closest to August 15, Assumption Day, a national holiday that kicks off summer vacation in Italy. Rome empties out; most places other than tourist spots close for the next two weeks. It may seem strange to serve such a heavy dish during the hottest part of the year, but this kind of one-pot meal is perfect because it can be made ahead of time, sits well, and is best eaten at room temperature.

Traditionally, this dish is served after Fettuccine con Rigaje di Pollo. Rigaje *is Roman dialect for chicken innards; the pasta is served with a sauce made from all of the bird's organs, stewed in tomato.*

The chickens we use at the RSFP come from Siena, through our purveyor Lo Spicchio. They are organic and, at almost 40 euros per bird, expensive, but our kitchen budget can accommodate the cost, since we tend to serve meat infrequently, especially during the summer months.

The first few times I made this dish in Rome, I removed all of the chicken fat that rose to the top, but after spending a few summers here and eating it in local trattorie, *I started to serve it the way the Romans do—always plated with tons of that delicious orange grease!—the perfect sauce to mop up with a* scarpetta, *the heel of a loaf of bread.*

> 1 (4 lb / 1.8 kg) whole chicken, cut into 8 bone-in pieces, seasoned
>   at least 6 hours in advance
> 2 tbsp kosher salt, plus additional for seasoning
> 1 tbsp olive oil
> 3 tbsp minced prosciutto fat or pancetta
> 2 large red bell peppers, deseeded and cut into 2-inch (5-cm) tiles
> 2 small red onions, peeled and thinly sliced
> 2 cloves garlic, peeled and smashed
> 2 sprigs rosemary, picked
> 2 sprigs marjoram, picked
> ¾ cup (180 ml) dry white wine
> 1 (28 oz / 794 g) can whole San Marzano—style tomatoes, crushed
>   by hand, liquid reserved

Season the chicken pieces with salt and let them rest in the refrigerator for at least 6 hours and up to overnight.

When you are ready to cook, heat a large pan (with a lid) that can fit all of the chicken pieces. Add the olive oil and minced prosciutto fat or pancetta. The olive oil is important because it will help the prosciutto fat or pancetta render without scorching.

Pat the chicken dry with paper towels. When the prosciutto fat has fully rendered, carefully add the chicken to the pan. It is important to brown the chicken, in batches, over medium heat. (Overcrowding the pan will drop the temperature and cause the meat to be steamed, resulting in poor browning. Also, be careful to control the heat during the browning process. You will build the sauce in this same pan, so you must be vigilant not to scorch the bottom.)

Once all the chicken has been browned, remove to a plate to rest while you make the sauce. Leave all the fat in the pan and keep it at medium heat. Add the bell peppers and sauté until just beginning to soften. Stir in the onions and garlic. Season with a pinch or two of salt. When all of the vegetables are softened, about 5 minutes, add the whole, picked herbs. When you can smell the aromatic herbs, deglaze the pan with the white wine, scraping up any browned bits from the bottom.

Once the smell of alcohol has subsided, add the crushed tomatoes and tomato liquid. When the tomato begins to boil, add the dark meat pieces back to the pan. Stir to combine and incorporate and bring the stew to a slow, steady simmer. Cover the pan with an offset lid. The lid encourages convection and more even cooking, and leaving a small space allows steam to escape as the sauce reduces and becomes more flavorful.

Stew the chicken pieces, stirring occasionally, until the meat is tender but not falling off the bone. Remove the lid and add in the breast pieces and simmer until just barely done, about 6 minutes. The white meat will carry over and finish cooking in the warm sauce. You may need to add water to keep the meat partially submerged during the cooking process.

Remove the pot from the heat. Taste the sauce for salt and adjust as necessary. After the chicken rests for a few minutes, you can degrease the sauce for a lighter presentation. I prefer to keep most of the grease in the dish.

The dish really benefits from resting for a few hours to allow the flavors to develop and seep deep into the meat. It is best served at room temperature, with lots of bread to mop up the sauce.

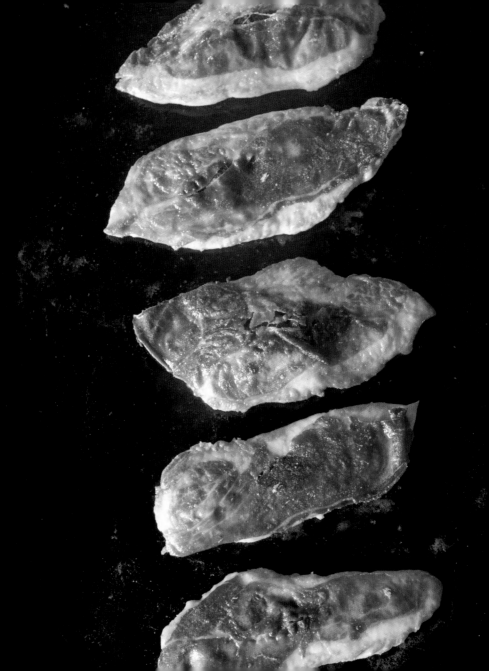

SALTIMBOCCA DI POLLO
CHICKEN SALTIMBOCCA

Serves 4

The classic Italian version of this dish, Saltimbocca alla romana, *is prepared with small scallops of veal, quickly cooked in butter with a slice of prosciutto and a leaf of sage, maybe with some white wine or Marsala. Many American chicken saltimbocca recipes stray very far from the original with gloppy brown sauces and melted cheese. With its simplicity, the RSFP version pays respect to the original.*

In the warmer months, we serve this dish simply grilled on our cast-iron piastra or griddle. In colder weather the meat is cooked in a pan and is served with a wine-based pan sauce. I use a combination of white wine and Marsala; the white wine helps to balance out the sweet Marsala. Saltimbocca *means "jumps in the mouth."*

> 4 lb (1.8 kg) boneless skinless chicken breasts and thighs
> Kosher salt, plus additional for seasoning
> 8 small sage leaves
> 4 thin slices of prosciutto, cut to fit each piece of chicken
> ½ cup (64 g) all-purpose flour
> 2 tbsp butter, plus additional if needed
> 1 tbsp olive oil
> ½ cup (120 ml) dry white wine
> ¼ cup (60 ml) dry Marsala wine
> Chicken broth or water

Use a meat mallet to gently flatten both the breast and leg pieces. Place one piece of meat inside a zip-lock bag (or cover the meat with plastic wrap on a cutting board) and gently and evenly pound the chicken until it is an even ¼-inch thickness. The thighs and legs can take a little more abuse than the breasts, but be careful not to tear them.

Season the cutlets with salt. Be careful not to overdo it; they are very thin pieces of meat and they will be covered with salty prosciutto.

Put two sage leaves on each piece of chicken, and then drape a piece of prosciutto over each piece, pressing gently so that the prosciutto adheres to the chicken. (I don't use toothpicks like most recipes because the sage is covered by the prosciutto; the

Roman style is to place the prosciutto first, then the sage leaf is pinned to the meat with a toothpick.)

Pour the flour into a large plate. Dredge the prepared chicken pieces in flour on both sides, shaking off any excess flour.

In a large sauté pan, melt the butter over medium heat along with the olive oil. Once the butter has foamed and subsided, but has not started to brown, add the breasts prosciutto-side down. Cook gently over medium heat—you do not want the prosciutto to burn. Flip the breasts after about 6 minutes, and cook on the other side for an additional 5 minutes until the breast is just cooked through. Remove the breasts to a plate to rest.

Sear the thighs in a similar manner, using additional butter as needed to grease the pan. When the thighs are cooked through, leave them in the pan and begin the sauce. (Although the thighs are cooked through, they need to be cooked longer to make them tender.) Add both wines to the pan and use a wooden utensil to scrape up any tasty brown bits from the bottom. Simmer until the smell of alcohol subsides, then add enough water or broth to submerge the thighs halfway. Simmer gently for about 20 minutes until the thigh meat is tender and can be pierced easily with a fork.

Return the breast to the pan, swirl to coat with the sauce, check the seasoning, and serve immediately. Be careful not to overcook the breast meat; it is already fully cooked. If the sauce is too thick, add water to thin it out. If the sauce is too thin, reduce slightly before adding the breast pieces in.

POLLO ALLA DIAVOLA

DEVIL'S-STYLE CHICKEN

Serves 4 to 6

Devil's-Style Chicken is a popular dish in the RSFP kitchen. We serve it hot in the colder months to warm everyone up; we also serve it in the summer months, but at room temperature.

Some alla diavola *recipes go overboard with vinegar, garlic, oregano, rosemary, mustard, paprika, and more. This stripped-down version with few seasonings allows the high-quality chicken to shine. A big squeeze of lemon is all it needs when served.*

This recipe features the Italian grilling technique al mattone (il mattone *is a brick) in which a foil-wrapped brick or heavy cast-iron pan is put on top of the chicken to help press it down evenly. This creates extra-crispy skin.*

The bird is prepared by removing the back and flattening it, a technique called "butterflying" in the U.S. This method allows the bird to cook evenly because the thighs are in direct contact with the heat. Italians cut poultry al mattone *the opposite way, by cutting right through the sternum. I prefer to cut the back out because it allows the thighs to cook before the breast is overcooked. Italians also leave the ribs in, which makes portioning the finished meat more difficult.*

At RSFP, we cook these on a large, cast-iron griddle called a piastra. *At home, a large cast-iron skillet works best; or, use a charcoal grill and cook the bird over indirect heat (build the fire to one side of the grill and cook the bird on the cooler side).*

My predecessor as chef, Chris Boswell, showed me this version of alla diavola. The first time we made it together we over-spiced the chicken and everyone in the kitchen was coughing because of the mace-like vapors in the air once the birds hit the grill.

> 1 (4 lb / 1.8 kg) whole chicken, butterflied, seasoned at least
>   12 hours in advance
> 2 tsp black peppercorns
> 1 tsp chili pepper flakes
> 2 tbsp kosher salt
> 3 tbsp olive oil
> 2 lemons, quartered, seeds removed

Ask your butcher to butterfly a chicken.

Finely grind the peppercorns and chili pepper in a spice grinder. Season the chicken first with salt then with the ground spices (or, as a shortcut, use a peppermill

and simply sprinkle the chili pepper on the chicken). Make sure to season all sides generously; this is not a subtle dish; it should be spicy and strong.

Let the chicken rest in the refrigerator, skin side up and uncovered, on a wire rack, for at least 12 and up to 24 hours, to allow the salt to be absorbed and the skin to dry slightly, ensuring crisp skin.

When you are ready to cook, wrap a brick in several layers of foil. Preheat the oven to 375°F (190°C) and heat a large cast-iron skillet or Dutch oven. Add the olive oil to the pan. If the chicken's skin has any moisture on it, be sure to first blot it dry with paper towels before putting the chicken in the pan. When the oil is warm, but not hot, add the chicken, skin side down. Once the chicken is in the pan, put the brick on top of it.

Controlling the temperature of the pan is very important. The chicken will be cooked almost entirely on one side. If the pan is too hot, the chicken will get too brown, or even burn to black, before the skin can evenly crisp up and the chicken has a chance to cook through. Keep the flame on medium-low/ low as you cook.

After 35 to 45 minutes of gentle crisping in the pan, the skin of the chicken should be a deep golden brown and the meat should be mostly opaque and no longer translucent. Remove the brick (it is no longer needed), flip the chicken to skin-side up, and put the pan in the oven for about 10 to 15 minutes, or until the chicken looks cooked and the thigh juices run clear when the skin is pierced. To be certain that the chicken is done, use an instant-read digital thermometer in the thickest part of the thigh; 165°F (75°C) is considered safe. I usually pull the chicken from the heat earlier, around 155°F (70°C), since the chicken continues to cook while it is resting.

Once the chicken is done, remove the chicken from the pan and allow it to rest on the cutting board for at least 25 minutes. To serve, cut the chicken in half, so that each breast can be sliced easily. Separate the legs and the thighs. Pile all the pieces onto a serving platter, and serve with lots and lots of lemon juice squeezed over the top.

QUAGLIE AL FORNO
OVEN-ROASTED QUAIL

———

Serves 4

We source our game birds from Siena, through our vendor Lo Spicchio. These organic birds are of the highest quality, and are always a treat for the interns who have not had the chance to work with this kind of specialty meat, as well as for the diners in our community who have never eaten quail or other small game birds.

American quail are usually available in two sizes, regular (4−5 oz / 110−140 g) or jumbo (6−7 oz / 170−200 g), and either whole or semi-boneless. For this recipe, I recommend semi-boneless jumbo quail, one per person. If you can only find the smaller size, allow two per person.

We almost never use butter here at RSFP for savory applications, but in this case I prefer butter to olive oil. The milk solids help the bird to brown during the short cooking time, and the fat also helps to baste the lean quail meat. Unlike like many chefs who suggest bringing the meat to room temperature before cooking, I encourage you to cook the quail still chilly from the refrigerator. This helps to ensure that the thickest part of the breast will remain pink and juicy. The cold skin also helps the melted butter to seize and adhere.

If your home oven is equipped with a convection fan, this is a great time to use it; it will help the skin to brown and crisp during the short cooking time. No fan? Use the broiler for the last few minutes of the cooking time to ensure that burnished skin.

> 4 jumbo quails, seasoned 2 to 6 hours in advance
> 2 tsp kosher salt
> Coarsely ground black pepper
> 4 small sprigs sage
> 2 sprigs rosemary, cut in half
> 2 small lemons, cut into quarters
> 3 tbsp butter, melted and held at room temperature

A few hours before you are ready to cook them, salt and pepper the quail all over, including inside the cavities. Stuff each bird with one sprig of sage, half a sprig of rosemary, and a quarter of a lemon, squeezing the lemon as you insert it into the cavity. Tie the quail's legs together to help seal the aromatic ingredients in the cavity. Put the quail in the refrigerator to rest for a few hours. (Seasoning the quail for longer than 6 hours is unnecessary; the birds are very small and the meat is delicate, so the seasoning does not need much time to penetrate.) Leave the tray uncovered so the skin has a chance to dry out. The dry skin will get crispier when roasted.

When you are ready to cook, preheat the oven to 500°F (260°C). If you have a convection fan in the oven, turn it on. Arrange the quail on a roasting tray. It is important that the quail are not placed too close together on the pan. Leaving ample space in between them will ensure even browning.

Use a brush to paint the birds on all sides with melted butter.

Roast the birds for about 12 to 15 minutes, until the breast has just firmed up and is still pink. The target internal temperature is around 155°F (70°C), but I usually choose not to use a thermometer; the bird is so small and lean that it can overcook quickly. This is more of a common sense judgment: "If it looks done, it is done." A quail is unlike a large chicken that can appear cooked on the outside but could be raw in the middle.

After 12 to 15 minutes, if the birds are still pale, use the broiler on high to brown the skin. Do not walk away while broiling—the skin can burn quickly.

Remove the pan from the oven and remove the quail to a plate to rest for about 2 minutes. Serve warm with the remaining lemon wedges.

TACCHINO RIPIENO
DEL GIORNO DEL RINGRAZIAMENTO
STUFFED TURKEY FOR THANKSGIVING

Serves 10 to 12

Thanksgiving dinner is one of the most beloved food events at the Academy. The Fellows, who arrive in September for an eleven-month stay, are just starting to get homesick for America when Thanksgiving comes around. The kitchen also looks forward to the holiday as a chance to cook something other than Italian food. Perhaps the biggest fans of this meal are the Academy staff, who are treated to the Thanksgiving spread for lunch the next day. In the days following Thanksgiving, the panino *sold at the bar is the classic leftover sandwich of turkey, stuffing, and cranberry sauce (*panino tacchino!*).*

We order ten to twelve turkeys, and then hold a "beauty contest" to pick out the biggest, most attractive bird. This turkey is then roasted whole, and plated on a silver platter on a bed of herbs and fruit from the garden. As a kickoff to the feast, two nominated Fellows wheel the show bird around to great applause in the dining room.

The Thanksgiving meal is usually served to about 120 people, the capacity of our dining room. Since we cannot cook twelve whole turkeys at once in our small ovens, we use an alternative technique: The white meat and the dark meat are cooked separately, in two different ways. Using this method, the turkey can be prepared ahead of time in stages, and there are no large tubs of brine to contend with. And, because dark meat and white meat require different cooking times, the result is even better than the classic method.

This is a big project; preparations should begin two or three days before Thanksgiving. If you are not comfortable breaking down a turkey, have your butcher do it for you.

1 (10 lb / 4.5 kg) turkey: 2 boneless, skin-on breasts with tenderloin; 2 bone-in, skin-on legs/thighs; bones, wings, and neck reserved for broth; giblets reserved for gravy

For the stuffed breasts:
3 tbsp kosher salt
1 tbsp coarsely ground black pepper
1 recipe Sage Sausage (page 125)
2 tbsp olive oil

For the braised legs:
3 tbsp olive oil
2 onions, peeled and quartered
3 carrots, peeled and cut into 3-inch (7.5-cm) chunks
3 celery stalks, cut into 3-inch (7.5-cm) chunks
1 fennel bulb, quartered
2 fresh bay leaves
6 sprigs thyme
4 cloves garlic, peeled
½ bottle white wine
Roasted turkey broth or water
1 recipe Salsa Gravy or Il Gravy (page 179)

Preheat the oven to 350°F (175°C).

Roast the reserved turkey bones, wings, and neck for about 30 minutes or until they are deeply browned. Put them in a pot and cover with water. Bring to a boil, then reduce the heat to a simmer. For maximum flavor, simmer the broth for about 6 hours, skimming occasionally. Strain and reserve in the refrigerator until needed.

Take each skin-on breast and lay it on a cutting board. Cut the breast horizontally, almost all the way through. Open the flap of meat like a book. Place the meat inside a plastic zip-lock bag or cover the meat with plastic wrap, and on the cutting board, gently and evenly pound the turkey until it is an even ½-inch (1-cm) thickness. (Be careful not to make a hole in the meat with the mallet. If the tenderloin falls off during the pounding process, lay it on the inside of the flattened turkey breast.)

Take each skin-on breast and lay it on a cutting board. Cut the breast horizontally, almost all the way through. Open the flap of meat like a book. Place the meat inside a plastic zip-lock bag or cover the meat with plastic wrap, and on the cutting board, gently and evenly pound the turkey until it is an even ½-inch (1-cm) thickness. (Be careful not to make a hole in the meat with the mallet. If the tenderloin falls off during the pounding process, lay it on the inside of the flattened turkey breast.)

Once both breasts are prepared this way, season the inside gently with salt and pepper. Be careful not to over-season—highly seasoned sausage meat will be added later. Smear a thin, even layer of the sage sausage on the part of the breast that is facing up. Be sure to cover the breast all the way to the edge with the filling. Roll the meat up into a nice, even log, starting from the edge of the meat that is closest to you. The meat and sausage should roll up into a pinwheel. Pull and adjust the skin around the outside so that it completely covers the roll, with the seam at the bottom. Season the outside of the meat log with salt and pepper, allow it to sit for a few minutes to absorb the seasoning, then rub with the oil. Use butcher's twine to tie the roast at 1-inch (2.5-cm) intervals. Allow to rest in the refrigerator for a few hours while the turkey legs cook, or up to overnight.

To cook the legs: Brown the two turkey legs in the olive oil in a large Dutch oven. Be careful to control the temperature—if the pan scorches it could ruin the braising liquid. When the legs are golden brown on all sides, remove them from the pan, leaving any fat behind.

Next, sauté the vegetables and aromatics in the remaining fat until golden brown. The vegetables do not need to be fully cooked; you just want the added flavor from the caramelizing. When the vegetables are nice and brown, carefully deglaze the pan with the white wine, scraping up any brown bits. Add the legs back to the pot, skin side up, and then add the prepared turkey broth or water until the legs are halfway submerged.

Bring the pot to a simmer, cover with a lid, and put in the oven. (If you don't have a Dutch oven with a lid, you can use a deep roasting pan covered with foil.) After about 30 minutes, remove the cover. Then, every 10 or 15 minutes while the meat is cooking, flip the legs over. This method of glazing and then flipping the meat helps to give a deep, rich flavor to the broth. Roast in the oven until the meat is tender and just beginning to fall away from the bone. This should take 1 to 1½ hours.

Remove the pan from the oven, and allow the turkey to cool in its liquid at room temperature. Using your hands, pull the meat from the bones in the largest possible pieces. Discard the soft, cooked skin and bones. Strain the braising liquid and pour it over the pulled meat. For full flavor, allow the meat to rest overnight in its broth in the refrigerator. (As an added bonus, after the meat has chilled overnight, the dish will be easier to degrease because the fat will rise to the top and solidify.)

To cook the breasts: One hour before you are ready to serve dinner, remove the turkey breasts from the refrigerator and preheat the oven to 350°F (175°C). Roast the breasts on a rack in a roasting pan for about 35 to 40 minutes, or until the internal temperature reaches 165°F (75°C).

While the breasts are roasting, gently reheat the pulled leg meat in its broth. To serve, give each plate a spoonful of the braised leg meat with some of its juice, and a few slices of the sausage-filled turkey rolls. If you find the turkey log slices are too cool after resting, smother with piping hot gravy.

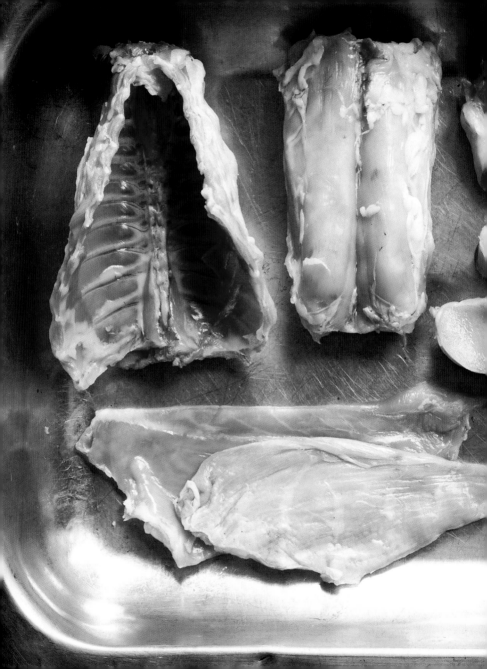

RABBIT

CONIGLIO ALLA GRIGLIA CON SALSA DI OLIVE

GRILLED RABBIT WITH OLIVE SALSA

———

Serves 4 to 6

This rabbit dish has no sauce other than a tasty olive tapenade-type relish. It's a light dish for warm weather, and delicious eaten at room temperature, like grilled chicken; in fact, chicken can be used instead of rabbit.

> 1 (3 lb /1.4 kg) rabbit or chicken, cut into 8 pieces,
>   marinated about 12 hours in advance
> 1 tbsp kosher salt
> 1 tsp dried oregano
> A pinch of chili pepper flakes
> 3 tbsp olive oil, plus additional for the salsa
> ½ red onion, peeled, cut into small dice, and submerged in
>   red wine vinegar
> ½ bunch Italian parsley, picked and chopped
> 1 cup (200 g) large green olives, pitted and chopped
> 2–3 lemons, zested

About 12 hours in advance, toss the rabbit pieces in a bowl first with salt, then oregano and chili pepper, then oil. Cover the bowl and refrigerate.

When you are ready to cook, light the grill and put on a medium flame. (If you don't have a grill, a stovetop grill pan or a large cast-iron pan will work just as well.)

While the grill is heating, make the salsa. Drain the marinated onions (reserve the vinegar to use in salad dressing) and mix them with the parsley, olives, and lemon zest. Add olive oil just until the mixture glistens.

Grill the rabbit pieces until lightly charred on the outside, removing the pieces from the grill as they are done. (The rabbit has been cut into eight pieces so that all the pieces will be done at about the same time.)

When all the meat is cooked through and nicely charred, remove to a platter and garnish with the herby salsa. If the plate looks a little dry, finish with a generous glug of olive oil.

CONIGLIO ALLA CACCIATORA
HUNTER'S-STYLE RABBIT

Serves 4 to 6

This dish is often served at the workers lunch, and always in bianco, *without tomato. Chicken may be used instead of rabbit.*

> 1 (3 lb / 1.4 kg) rabbit or chicken, cut into 8 pieces, salted about
>   12 hours in advance
> 1 tbsp plus a pinch of kosher salt, plus additional for seasoning
> 3 tbsp olive oil
> 3 cloves garlic, peeled and smashed
> 1 medium red onion, peeled and sliced
> 2 sprigs rosemary, picked and roughly chopped
> 1 sprig sage or thyme, picked and roughly chopped
> 2 salt-packed anchovies, soaked, deboned, and rinsed
> A pinch of chili pepper flakes
> 1 tablespoon salt-packed capers, purged of salt (see below) and
>   roughly chopped
> 1 cup (240 ml) white wine
> 3 tbsp white wine vinegar
> 1 quart (960 ml) chicken broth or water
> 10—12 oil-cured black olives with pits, such as Gaeta

Salt the rabbit pieces about 12 hours in advance of cooking.

Purge the capers by rinsing off the excess salt, then simmer them in water for about 2 minutes. (Do not boil.) Drain, add fresh water, and simmer the capers for another 2 minutes. Drain and set aside.

When you are ready to cook, heat the 3 tablespoons of olive oil over medium heat in a large, low-sided wide pan (with a lid), that can fit all the rabbit pieces. When the oil shimmers, add the pieces and brown on all sides. Be sure to control the heat so the rabbit does not burn, but is evenly light golden brown on all sides and the pan is not scorched. The meat should be seared but not cooked all the way through.

As they finish cooking, remove the pieces to a plate. In the same pan, add the smashed garlic and onion along with a pinch of salt, and cook until soft and translucent but not colored.

To the same pan, add the herbs, anchovies, chili pepper, and capers, and cook until the anchovy is melted and the *soffritto* is softened. Deglaze the pan with the wine and reduce until the smell of alcohol has subsided. Add the dark meat pieces back to the pan, followed by the vinegar and the broth.

Simmer gently, partially covered, for about 40 minutes until the meat is tender but not falling off the bone. Add in the pieces of white meat and the whole olives in the final 10 minutes of cooking, being careful not to overcook.

Taste the sauce and adjust the salt, chili pepper, and vinegar. If the sauce is too loose, remove the meat and reduce the liquid until thickened. If too thick, add water and adjust the seasoning again.

CONIGLIO FRITTO ALLA TOSCANA
TUSCAN-STYLE FRIED RABBIT

Serves 4 to 6

This dish originated with the Tuscan Jewish population. The spices are reminiscent of Middle Eastern flavors.

Traditionally the rabbit (or chicken, if you prefer) is marinated in lemon juice and garlic overnight and then floured and fried, but I find that the highly acidic lemon marinade makes the meat tough, so I go a different route to flavor and season the meat. I braise the dark meat, but not the white, then let them both rest in the marinade overnight, before frying them.

Although this recipe takes a few days to complete, the time investment is worth it, turning often bland and overcooked rabbit into something special.

> 1 (3 lb / 1.4 kg) rabbit or chicken, cut into 8 pieces,
>   salted 12 hours in advance
> 1 tbsp kosher salt
> 3 tbsp olive oil, plus additional for frying
> 3 cups (720 ml) rabbit broth (made from reserved rabbit
>   bones from the butcher, or chicken broth, or water
> 1 cup (240 ml) white wine
> 2–3 lemons, juiced and zested with a vegetable peeler
> 6 sprigs of thyme
> 6 cloves garlic, unpeeled
> 1 tsp whole black peppercorns
> 1 cinnamon stick, broken in half
> A pinch of grated nutmeg
> Olive oil for frying
> 1 cup (128 g) all-purpose flour
> 4 eggs, whisked
> 1 lemon, cut into wedges
> Coarsely ground black pepper

Salt the rabbit pieces about 12 hours in advance.

When you are ready to cook, heat the 3 tablespoons of olive oil over medium heat in a large, low-sided wide pan (with a lid), that can fit all the rabbit pieces. When the oil shimmers, add the pieces and brown on all sides. Be sure to control the heat so the rabbit does not burn, but is evenly light golden brown on all sides and the pan is not scorched. The meat should be seared but not cooked all the way through.

As they finish cooking, remove the pieces to a plate.

Put the broth or water, white wine, lemon juice and zest, thyme, garlic, peppercorns, cinnamon stick, and nutmeg in a saucepan, and heat to a simmer.

Arrange the dark-meat rabbit pieces in a large baking dish, and pour the warm braise over the seared meat. The liquid should not quite cover the meat. Cover the dish tightly with aluminum foil and braise in a 300°F (150°C) oven for 45 minutes to an hour, until the meat is tender but not quite falling off the bone. A paring knife should easily slide in and out of the thickest part of the meat on the thigh.

Remove from the oven and allow the meat to cool on the countertop in its liquid. Add the reserved seared white meat pieces to the liquid, cover with plastic wrap, and refrigerate overnight.

The next day, gently warm up the pan in a 250°F (120°C) oven until the broth has liquefied. Remove the meat pieces and allow them to drain on paper towels, discarding any bits of herbs and seasonings.

Heat about 2 inches (5 cm) of olive oil in a medium pan until it reaches 375°F (190°C). Toss the rabbit pieces first in flour, knocking off any excess, then in the beaten egg. Allow extra egg to drip away. Fry the pieces in the oil for 4 to 6 minutes, depending on the size, until the outside is golden brown. (Remember: The meat is fully cooked, this step is just to reheat the meat all the way through and crisp up the outside.)

As each piece is removed from the pan, sprinkle with salt. Serve hot or at room temperature with lemon wedges.

CURED,
GROUND
& BRINED

PROSCIUTTO COTTO
COOKED HAM

Think: homemade deli ham. Prosciutto cotto *is usually made with the lean rear leg of the pig, which is skinned, deboned, brined, and either roasted or poached.*

A product that is injected and cured with a brine, and then cooked, is what is referred to as a "city ham" (vs. a "country ham," which is dry-cured, not cooked, and often smoked). Hams can be cured on or off the bone. I prefer boneless hams because of the shorter cure time and easier cooking and slicing. This ham should be served cold or at room temperature; it would taste too salty if served hot.

Brining is the natural and extremely easy solution to prevent meat from drying out. Brining works like this: Salted water is injected into meat, or meat is soaked in a brine, and by the process of osmosis, the salt enters and actually changes the shape of the meat proteins to allow them to hold more juice than un-brined meat. Brining is most often used on lean meats, such as pork, chicken, or turkey, to make the finished dish more juicy than it would have been if not brined.

In this recipe, the pork is injected with a flavorful brine, along with sodium nitrate (AKA Pink salt #1, or Instacure #1, or Prague powder #1). Curing salt designated #1 is used for fresh cured products. It contains 6.25% sodium nitrate and 93.75% table salt. It is mixed in this way and colored pink for safety reasons; pure sodium nitrate is toxic. The nitrate gives the ham its pink color and adds to that cured hot-doggy, hammy flavor; and it protects against the growth of botulism.

I have been making prosciutto cotto *my whole career, but I honed the recipe after my time at BKLYN Larder, where I learned the techniques used there. I have continued to build upon the recipe after years of testing, to arrive at the recipe you see here.*

The use of an injection needle is not 100% necessary, but very highly recommended. It will speed up the brine time, and ensure that the curing salt penetrates all parts of the meat. If the brine does not penetrate throughout, the meat ends up with what's called a bulls-eye, or gray splotch, usually deep within the meat, that was not reached by the pink salt. If you do not have a brining needle (they're easy to find online), you will need to double the length of the time the meat is brined.

This may seem like a big investment in time, labor, and supplies, but prosciutto cotto *is perfect for large gatherings. Also, the meat has a long shelf life (in the fridge) because of the curing salt, so you can use it over a few weeks!*

Ask your butcher for a rear pork leg, without the shank muscles (the tubular muscles closest to the pig foot which are full of sinew and not great for ham). They should have just about a 1-inch (2.5-cm) layer of fat. Have the butcher clean all visible sinew, veins, and silverskin from the inside of the leg—the cleaner the meat the better. You will need exactly 6 pounds of pork for this recipe to work well. Feel free to use this recipe on other cuts of pork, such as boneless shoulder. (You may have to increase the cooking time because of all the tough connective tissue in the shoulder.)

Over many years of testing, I have discovered that to my taste, using just a few vegetables is ideal; the ham tastes like ham, not vegetable broth. The Cinta Sinese pork we use at RSFP is so beautiful, I try to accent it, not hide it. You can change up the spices any way you like; use brown sugar, cinnamon, clove—or even a splash of bourbon!— depending on what you like.

> 2 gallons (about 7.5 liters) water
> 1 oz (30 g) Curing Salt #1
> 8.8 oz (250 g) granulated sugar, or brown or turbinado sugar if preferred
> 13 oz (375 g) kosher salt
> 3 small bay leaves, fresh or dried
> 1 tbsp whole black peppercorns, plus grindings of pepper for seasoning
> 2 whole star anise
> 2 whole dried chili peppers or 2 tsp chili pepper flakes
> 2 white onions, peeled and thinly sliced
> 1 celery stalk, thinly sliced
> 1 carrot, peeled and thinly sliced
> 1 (6 lb / 2.7 kg) boneless, skinless pork leg, shank muscles removed, fat
>   trimmed to about 1 inch, cleaned of silverskin, veins, and sinew, kept
>   cold at all times
> Coarsely ground black pepper

Make the brine: Put the kosher salt, curing salt, sugar, bay leaves, peppercorns, star anise, chili pepper, and sliced vegetables into a large pot with the water, bring to a boil, then reduce the heat and simmer no more than 10 minutes. (You don't want to reduce the brine and make it too strong; the salts and the sugars only need to melt and the vegetables only need to wilt.) Cool the brine until it is ice-cold. You can use ice packs to bring the temperature down rapidly, or cool the liquid to room temperature on your countertop and then refrigerate it overnight.

The brine MUST be ice-cold before adding the meat to it.

Put the cold pork leg in a large, lidded container (that you can fit in your refrigerator!) and pour the ice-cold brine over it. Use the injection needle to inject the brine every inch or so. You should inject every surface of the meat, so that the meat is swollen with brine. (You won't inject all of the brine; some will be left for soaking the meat.) Brine the meat in the coldest part of the fridge, usually the bottom (cold sinks) for 5 days. (If not injecting the brine, but simply soaking the meat in it, the meat must brine for at least 10 days.) You should "overhaul," or flip and agitate the ham and its brine every day. This will ensure the brine is moving freely all over the meat.

After 5 days (or 10 days, if you are using the soaking method), remove the ham from its brine. Allow it to rest in the refrigerator on a rack for at least 3 hours, to allow the action of osmosis to evenly redistribute the brine solution throughout the ham.

When you're ready to cook, preheat the oven to 275°F (135°C). Blot the meat dry with paper towels, being careful to discard any remaining vegetables or spices from the brine. Using strong kitchen twine, tie the ham at about 1-inch intervals into a football-like shape with the fat on the outside. Liberally coat all sides of the tied roast with freshly ground pepper.

Put the pork on a rack in a roasting pan, and cook until an internal temperature of 120°F (50°C) is reached, about 90 minutes to 2 hours. At this point, raise the temperature of the oven to 475°F (250°C) and roast until the internal temp reaches 135°F (60°C), about 20 to 30 minutes depending on your oven. Keep an eye on the meat during this stage, as it can burn easily at this high temperature. Remove from the oven and cool completely before slicing and/or storing.

PANCETTA FRESCA

QUICK-CURED PORK BELLY

Think unsmoked bacon. Pancetta fresca *is a cheaper and more convenient replacement for often very expensive imported pancetta, and is much better than the commercial pancetta that is widely available in the U.S. It can be cooked whole, diced and rendered crispy (for your favorite pasta, salad, etc.). Unlike* guanciale *(page 119), this does not need to age or hang.*

> 1 fresh pork belly, skin on
> Kosher salt
> Curing Salt #1

Use any size fresh pork belly with the skin on. Use a sharp knife to square it off, saving the scraps for broth or sausage. Weigh the trimmed belly. Calculate 1½% kosher salt by weight and 1 gram of Curing Salt #1 per pound. Mix the two salts together and apply evenly to all sides of the belly. Allow to rest in the refrigerator for at least 2 days, flipping the belly over several times.

At this point, the belly can be cooked whole in a large, covered baking dish in the oven at 300°F (150°C) until knife-tender, about 2 hours. When cool, the skin can be removed easily by pulling it away from the meat. The pancetta is now ready to be diced and stored, refrigerated, until needed. Use within 2 weeks. It freezes well.

GUANCIALE

CURED PORK JOWL

———

Pork jowls can be hard to find, even at specialty butchers, but are worth seeking out—
they are an important part of Roman cuisine and provide a unique flavor and tons of fat!
Guanciale is the backbone of many famous Roman pastas, like Carbonara. Pancetta is a
great substitute.

Curing Salt #2 is used on items that are dry cured over an extended period of time,
like salumi or cured meats. (The sodium nitrate in the cure breaks down over time to
sodium nitrite and that is then broken down to nitric oxide, which acts as an oxidizing
agent to prevent botulism.)

Pork jowls
Kosher salt
Curing Salt #2
Black pepper

Calculate 1½% kosher salt by weight, and 1 gram of Curing Salt #2 per pound. Mix
the two salts together and apply evenly to all sides of the jowls. Cure the jowls for
a week, in the refrigerator on an uncovered tray, flipping them daily. After the jowls
have cured for a week, brush off the excess salt, and coat them liberally with coarse
black pepper. Punch a small hole in one end of the cheek, thread a string through it,
and hang the jowls in a cool, moist place, such as a basement (50–60°F / 10–15°C
and about 60% humidity), for approximately 4 weeks until they lose about 30% of
their weight.

POLPETTONE RIPIENO

STUFFED MEATLOAF

Serves 8

I grew up with my mom making meatloaf stuffed with whole sausages and hard-boiled eggs. In Rome, I saw stuffed meatloaf for the first time at the pizzeria Da Simone, the neighborhood pizza spot near the Academy; it was made with ground veal, ham, and cheese, and smothered in brown gravy.

For this and all of the ground meat recipes in this book, it is always better to have your butcher grind fresh cuts of meat, rather than buying pre-ground products, which can sometimes contain unsavory bits of cartilage and sinew. It can cost a bit more, but the results will be better.

In this recipe, I use fresh breadcrumbs soaked in milk instead of the traditional fine dried breadcrumbs. The fresh bread holds more moisture, making the meatloaf juicer.

> 4 cups (120 grams) spinach, cleaned dried, large stems discarded
> 1 tbsp kosher salt, plus additional for spinach and seasoning
> ½ loaf day-old country bread (about 8 oz / 227 g), crust removed,
>   diced into ¼-inch (.5-cm) cubes
> 1 cup (240 ml) milk
> 3 eggs, whisked
> ½ cup (125 g) ricotta cheese
> 1 lb (454 g) ground beef
> 1 lb (454 g) ground fatty pork
> ½ tsp coarsely ground black pepper
> ½ tsp dried oregano
> A pinch of chili pepper flakes
> About 3/4 cups (58 g) grated pecorino Romano
> 2 cloves garlic, peeled, smashed and made into a paste
> ½ bunch parsley, picked and finely chopped
> 8 thin slices prosciutto cotto or deli ham
> 8 thin slices provolone picante or other cheese, such as cheddar
>   or Swiss

Preheat the oven to 350°F (175°C).

Boil the cleaned spinach in lightly salted water in a medium saucepan until the leaves are tender, about 45 seconds. Remove from the water with a slotted spoon, and spread out on a baking sheet to cool. Once cool, ball up the spinach and squeeze out excess water. Chop roughly, taste for salt, and set aside.

In a bowl, combine the diced bread, milk, eggs, and ricotta. Mix well and allow the mix to hydrate while you prepare the meat, about 30 minutes.

Thoroughly mix the beef and pork with the 2 tablespoons of salt, then the dried spices, pecorino, garlic, and parsley.

The bread mix should have absorbed most of the liquid. Using your hands, squeeze the bread to remove excess milk, and work the bread into a fine paste. Allow the paste to drain in a colander for 20 minutes. (If the bread holds onto too much liquid, the meat mixture will be loose and sticky and the meatloaf will not maintain its shape during baking.)

Combine the squeezed breadcrumbs in the bowl with the meat mixture. Mix until the bread and meat mixture become homogeneous. Pinch off a small piece of the meatloaf mix and fry it gently in a small sauté pan. Test for seasoning, adjusting the salt and spices if necessary.

Turn out the meatloaf mix on a piece of parchment paper. Form the meat into a rectangle, about 8 x 12 inches (about 20 x 30 cm) and about ½-inch (1-cm) thick. Layer the cheese, then the ham, then the spinach, evenly over the surface of the meat, leaving about a 1-inch (2.5-cm) border on the shorter sides.

Using the parchment paper, roll the meat into a log, making sure to keep all the cheese, ham, and spinach in the center. Round off the ends with your hands to make sure the filling stays inside during baking.

Transfer the meatloaf to a parchment-lined baking sheet, and bake in a preheated oven for about 1 hour and 15 minutes. The meatloaf will cook faster than you think because the filling is less dense than the meat. The internal temperature should be around 150–160°F (65–70°C).

Allow the meatloaf to cool for at least 25 minutes before slicing it with a serrated knife. Serve with brown gravy made from the pan drippings, or even a little bit of simple tomato sauce.

SALSICCIA DI MAIALE

PORK SAUSAGE

Serves 6 to 8

This recipe can be used for both sausage patties and cased sausages. There are many ways to vary the basic recipe (see below).

> 1 lb (454 g) pork shoulder, finely ground
> 1 lb (454 g) pork belly, medium ground
> 2 tsp kosher salt
> 2 cloves garlic, smashed and finely minced
> A pinch of chili pepper flakes (more for spicy sausage)
> 1 tsp fennel seeds
> ½ cup (120 ml) white wine

Combine all the ingredients in a bowl, using your hands. Be careful not to over-mix, or the sausage can become tough when cooked. Cook off a small amount of the sausage to check for seasoning before storing.

For Broccoli Rabe and Provolone Sausage, add to the basic recipe 2 cups (400 g) blanched, squeezed, and chopped broccoli rabe and 1 cup (150 g) diced, young provolone.

For Tomato and Mozzarella Sausage, omit the fennel seeds from the basic recipe, replace the white wine with ice-cold water, fold in four peeled, seeded, and diced tomatoes or a drained 28-ounce (794 g) can of peeled, diced tomatoes, 1 cup (30 g) of fresh chopped basil leaves, and 1 pound (454 g) of diced, drained, low-moisture mozzarella.

For Sage Breakfast Sausage, omit the fennel seeds from the basic recipe and replace the white wine with ice-cold water. Add 1 tablespoon of ground black pepper, ½ teaspoon ground cloves, ½ teaspoon dried thyme, and 1 teaspoon ground coriander. Substitute 3 teaspoons of Sage Salt (see page 181) for the 2 teaspoons of kosher salt. Some recipes for breakfast sausage include sugar or maple syrup in the ingredients, but to prevent the sugar from caramelizing and burning in the pan when cooked, I prefer to serve the cooked sausages with maple syrup on the side.

POLPETTINE DI AGNELLO

LAMB MEATBALLS

———

Serves 4 to 6

As delicious as pork and beef meatballs are, it's fun to change things up and use lamb as the main ingredient. I use a mix of lamb and pork since lamb by itself tends to be slightly gamey and lean. These meatballs are not cooked in sauce, but reminiscent of polpette alla piastra, the grilled meatballs that are popular all over Italy. In Rome, they're sometimes even called "hamburger"; in Sicily, these tender meatballs are sometimes grilled with lemon leaves and served with a sprinkle of lemon juice and dried oregano. Serve warm with a simple salad, a yogurt sauce with cucumbers, or pickled vegetables.

> 1 (1½ lb /680 g) lamb shoulder, finely ground
> 1 (½ lb / 227 g) pork belly, finely ground
> 2 tsp kosher salt
> A pinch of chili pepper flakes
> 1 tsp ground coriander
> 1 tsp dried oregano
> Zest of 1 large lemon
> 1 tsp coarsely ground black pepper
> ½ cup (120 ml) white wine
> 1½ cups (60 g) country white bread, crust removed, cut into
>   small dice, soaked in water and excess water squeezed out
> Olive oil
> 1 lemon, cut into 6 wedges

Combine all ingredients (except the olive oil) in a bowl, using your hands. Heat a large cast-iron skillet over a medium flame, and add enough olive oil to cover the bottom of the pan. When the oil shimmers, cook a small amount of the meatball mix to check it for seasoning before using.

For each *polpettina*, take a 1-ounce portion of meat and using your hands shape it into a ball. Add the meatballs to the pan and use a spatula to slightly flatten them; this will help cook them more evenly.

Brown each patty for about 4 minutes on each side, until golden brown and crispy. I prefer to serve these lamb meatballs at a medium temperature, rosy and pink throughout, but you can cook them well done, if you prefer. The fat from the pork belly will keep them from drying out. Serve with lemon wedges.

LEBERWURST

LIVERWURST

Serves 8 to 10

The intense flavor of beef liver is not for the faint of heart; it took a lot of adjustments to get this recipe just right. I wanted to develop a recipe that uses all the traditional seasonings and make something instantly recognizable as classic liverwurst, but mild enough to appeal to the community here at the Academy.

Although this recipe surely has Germanic roots, the up-front offal flavor is something that is decidedly Roman. Romans have a special affinity for the "fifth quarter" of the animal, the innards. The Ex-Mattatoio, a decommissioned slaughterhouse in Testaccio and now the site of a weekly farmers' market, inspired this recipe.

> 1 (1 lb / 454 g) beef liver, cleaned of veins and membranes, diced
> into 1-inch (2.5-cm) pieces
> 1½ tbsp kosher salt
> ½ lb (227 g) pancetta or bacon, thinly sliced and diced, or ground
> Olive oil
> ½ lb (227 g) pork, finely ground
> 3 tbsp butter
> 1 medium red onion, peeled and cut into small dice
> 2 cloves garlic, minced
> 2 tsp coarsely ground black pepper
> ¼ tsp grated nutmeg, bought whole and freshly grated
> ¼ tsp ground allspice, berries bought whole and freshly ground
> 1 tsp ground clove, bought whole and freshly ground
> 2 tbsp barrel-aged grappa or brandy

Preheat the oven to 300°F (150°C).

Pat the liver dry with paper towels and season with salt.

In a large, thick-bottomed pan over medium-low heat, render the pancetta with a few drops of olive oil. Do not allow the pancetta to brown or get crispy; you just want to soften it and render the fat.

Once the pancetta is rendered, add in the ground pork, breaking it up with a spoon. Again, control the heat to prevent browning.

Add the butter. As soon as it melts, add the onion, garlic, and ground spices. Add in the grappa and cook for a few minutes. Pour this mixture into a large dish and allow to cool slightly.

In a blender, puree the liver with the room-temperature pancetta and pork mixture until it is smooth. (You can use a food processor, but I use a blender because it is more powerful.) I prefer liverwurst with a rustic texture, but if you want it to be very smooth, you can pass the mixture through a sieve.

Line a terrine mold, small baking dish, or loaf pan with plastic wrap. Adding a few drops of water or oil to the pan before putting in the plastic wrap will help it to adhere to the sides. Make sure there is enough overhang on the plastic to cover the top. Spoon the liverwurst mixture into the mold, tap on the countertop to remove air bubbles, and cover the top with the overhanging plastic. Cover tightly with foil.

Place the terrine in a high-sided roasting pan and add very hot tap water to come halfway up the sides of the terrine. Put the pan in the oven and bake until the interior of the liverwurst reaches 145°F (65°C), about 1 hour, up to 90 minutes.

When the internal temp is reached, remove the pan from the oven and remove the terrine from the water bath. Refrigerate for at least 2 days to allow the flavors to mature and develop.

The mix may be served in rough slices or simply smeared on toasts, but I prefer to take some of the cooked terrine and put it once again in the blender. This step makes the mix airy and delicate. Serve with pickles, sliced onion, mustard, or simply with some fresh black pepper.

TERRINA DI CAMPAGNA

COUNTRY TERRINE

Serves 8 to 10 as a terrine, or yields enough stuffing for 4 to 6 small birds

This is a great way for us to use up the scraps and innards from the many butchering projects in the RSFP kitchen. Making a terrine is a fun and practical project for those with meat grinders or a KitchenAid with a grinding attachment, but it can also be made with some help from your butcher.

We serve the pâté in slices, with mustard or pickled vegetables, and crostini. We also like to use it as a stuffing for chicken as well as roasted game birds, like guinea hen and squab. This recipe is adapted from the bible for all butchers and meat cooks, Cooking by Hand by Paul Bertolli.

The recipe for Pâté Spice makes more than the ½ teaspoon called for in this recipe; save the extra for future recipes.

Refrigerated, the pâté will keep for up to 2 weeks.

> 1½ lb (680 g) pork shoulder, ground
> ½ lb (227 g) pork belly, ground
> 4 oz (113 g) pork or poultry liver, finely chopped by hand
> ½ tsp Pâté Spice (page 181)
> 2 tbsp kosher salt
> 1 tsp coarsely ground black pepper
> ½ cup (75 g) white onions or shallots, peeled and finely chopped
> ½ bunch parsley, picked and chopped
> 3 cloves garlic, peeled, smashed, and minced into a paste
> 2 tbsp all-purpose flour
> 2 eggs
> 2 tbsp barrel-aged grappa or brandy
> 2 slices white bread, crusts removed and torn into small pieces
> ½ cup (120 ml) heavy cream

Preheat the oven to 300°F (150°C).

Combine the pork shoulder, pork belly, and liver with the ½ teaspoon of the spice mixture, the salt and pepper, and the aromatics. Allow the mixture to rest in the refrigerator while you prepare the panade, the mix that will help bind the terrine.

Mix the flour, eggs, grappa, bread, and cream in a bowl until the bread breaks down into a paste. Add it to the meat mixture. Stir thoroughly to combine, about 1 minute. The mixture should be sticky.

Take a small piece of the mixture and fry it in a sauté pan to check the seasoning. Adjust with salt, pepper, and pâté spice if necessary.

Line a terrine mold, small baking dish, or loaf pan with plastic wrap. Adding a few drops of water or oil to the pan before putting in the plastic wrap will help to adhere it to the sides. Make sure there is enough overhang on the plastic to cover the top.

Spoon the meat mixture into the terrine in small increments, pushing each addition down evenly to avoid air pockets. Once all of the meat is inside, give it one final press, then cover with the plastic wrap that is hanging over the sides of the terrine. Cover with a lid or foil.

Place the terrine in a high-sided roasting pan and add very hot tap water to come halfway up the sides of the terrine. Put the pan in the oven and bake until the interior of the pâté reaches 145°F (65°C), about 1 hour.

When the internal temperature is reached, remove the pan from the oven and remove the terrine from the water bath. Weigh the terrine down (a piece of cardboard cut to fit, topped with with a few small cans from your pantry, should do the job) and allow it to come to room temperature on the countertop.

Refrigerate, with the weight, for at least 24 hours, up to 4 days. The meat needs time to press and the flavors need to mature.

To unmold, run a knife around the outside edges of the terrine to break up any congealed fat, then use the plastic to lift out the loaf. Cut into slices, and serve at room temperature with mustard, pickled vegetables, and crostini.

CONSERVA DI MAIALE

POTTED PORK

Serves 8 to 10

This is another great way to use up meat scraps, or even better, to repurpose leftover cooked meat. We often make this with pork, or sometimes we'll pick the cooked meat from rabbit bones to make a tasty spread. If using cooked meat, simply use the food processor to puree the meat with the seasonings, while streaming in the melted fat or olive oil.

Refrigerated, the conserva, *if covered by a layer of fat, will keep indefinitely; if not covered by fat, it will keep about a week.*

>2 lb (907 g) skinless, boneless pork shoulder, diced
>>into 1½-inch (4-cm) pieces
>1 lb (454 g) skin-on pork belly, diced into 1½-inch (4-cm) pieces
>1 tbsp kosher salt
>1 tsp coarsely ground black pepper
>2 sprigs rosemary, picked and chopped
>3 fresh bay leaves
>4 cloves garlic, peeled
>1½ cups (360 ml) dry white wine
>Red wine vinegar

Preheat the oven to 275°F (135°C).

Mix the pork shoulder and belly with the salt and pepper in a bowl, and then put it into a baking dish that can hold all of the meat in a single layer.

Add the rosemary, bay leaves, and garlic cloves, and pour the white wine over the mixture. Cover the pan tightly with aluminum foil. (Do not let the meat touch the foil. If it does, either change the pan or put a sheet of parchment paper between the pork and the foil.)

Put the pan in the oven and braise slowly for about 3 hours, until the meat is falling apart. Uncover the pan and return to the oven for 20 more minutes, to allow extra moisture to evaporate and the flavors to intensify.

Pull the pan out and, with a slotted spoon, remove the solids to a bowl, reserving the fat and drippings in the pan.

Using a potato masher or two large forks, break the meat down until it is a chunky puree. Add in the reserved fat and pork liquid (you may not use all of it) and continue to break the meat down until it is a spreadable paste.

Check the seasoning, remembering that this will be served cold, so the seasoning must be more intense. Add the vinegar in small amounts until you achieve a nice acidity that balances the richness of the pork. Once the mixture is seasoned, pack it tightly into small jars or a dish, and cover the top with any remaining pork fat to seal and preserve the *conserva*. Serve chilled with crostini and pickled vegetables.

PÂTÉ DI FEGATINI
POULTRY LIVER SPREAD

Serves 6 to 8

This technique was taught to me by my mentor, Nate Appleman, when we were cooking at A16 in San Francisco; it has become a favorite in the RSFP kitchen. The recipe is flexible, because it is based on eyeballing the amounts of ingredients in descending order: for example, five parts liver, four parts onion, three parts capers, two parts herbs, one part anchovies. The recipe below is more specific, but it certainly can be modified. I also like to tweak the original recipe to be more like classic Jewish chopped liver, by using more onion and sage and leaving the mixture chunkier.

> 2 cups (420 g) poultry livers, cleaned and salted about 1 hour in advance
> 1 tbsp kosher salt plus additional for salting the fried herbs
> 4 tbsp olive oil, divided
> 1 cup (150 g) white onion, peeled and diced
> 4 sprigs rosemary, divided
> 4 sprigs sage, divided
> ½ cup (75 g) salted capers, purged of salt (see below), squeezed, and chopped
> 3 salted anchovies, purged of salt and filleted
> 1 tsp coarsely ground black pepper
> 1 cup (240 ml) dry white wine
> 1 cup (240 ml) dry or sweet Marsala or other sweet wine
> 3 tbsp cold butter, cubed
> Vegetable oil

Season the livers with salt. Allow to rest in the refrigerator for about 1 hour while you gather your ingredients and purge the capers.

Purge the capers by rinsing off the excess salt, then simmer them in water for about 2 minutes. (Do not boil.) Drain, add fresh water, and simmer the capers for another 2 minutes. Drain and set aside.

When you are ready to cook, take the livers out of the refrigerator and pat dry with paper towels. It is very important that the livers are dry, or they can violently spray oil when cooking.

In a wide sauté pan over medium-high heat, add 2 tablespoons of the olive oil. When the oil shimmers, carefully add the livers. Avoid overcrowding, or the livers will boil instead of sear, and will have an unappetizing gray color and flavor. In this step it is important to sear the livers without cooking them all the way through. They should remain rosy throughout, with a deep golden brown on the outside. Cook the livers in batches if your pan cannot hold them all at once. Be careful to control the heat so the bottom of the pan does not scorch. A lot of flavor will come from the brown bits that remain in the pan after searing—do not burn them.

Remove the seared livers to a plate and allow them to cool. In the same pan, add the remaining 2 tablespoons of olive oil and the diced onions. Sweat over very low heat, stirring constantly, until the onions are translucent and sweet.

Very finely chop two of the rosemary sprigs and two of the sprigs of sage and add to the pan, followed by the capers and anchovies. Season with black pepper and sweat the mix gently until softened.

Increase the heat to medium, then deglaze the pan with the wine and the Marsala, scraping up all the brown bits from the bottom. Once the smell of alcohol has subsided, scrape the mix out onto the plate with the livers and allow it to cool slightly.

Put the room-temperature livers, any accumulated juices, and the onion mixture in the food processor. As it is processing, drop in cubes of cold butter. You may not need the entire 3 tablespoons; stop adding butter when the mixture is glossy. You can process the mix until it is super-smooth (or pass it through a fine mesh if you want it incredibly smooth) or just pulse to combine for more of a "chopped liver" effect. Transfer mix to a bowl, cover with plastic, and let rest while you fry the garnish.

Pour about 1½ inches of vegetable oil in a small pot and heat it to about 350°F (175°C). Quickly fry the reserved sage and rosemary leaves separately, about 15 to 20 seconds each. As the herbs come out, put them on a paper towel–lined plate and season with a sprinkle of salt.

Check the liver spread for seasoning, adding more salt and pepper if needed. Crumble the fried herbs on top and serve with slices of fresh bread or toasts.

SIDE DISHES

POMODORI VERDI SOTT'ACETO
PICKLED GREEN TOMATOES

Makes 1 quart or enough for six sandwiches

This is a dish I developed for BKLYN Larder. I sold the marinated tomatoes by the pound and also used them on a sandwich, with wild arugula and mozzarella. The combination of the briny, marinated tomato, milky mozzarella, and peppery arugula on a soft but crispy long roll, was amazing. I also serve them alongside roasted meats and in salads.

At the Academy, I use the green tomatoes that drop to the ground in our garden, and also, at the end of the season, the many green tomatoes that remain on the vine. Use medium-size, round tomatoes; the larger ones may have too many juicy seeds and may fall apart when poaching; the smaller ones may be too unripe and too crunchy to eat. The top and bottom slices of tomato are mostly skin, and can be tough to eat. I prefer to reserve the pickled end pieces and chop them finely to use in relishes and salad dressings.

Strips of green bell pepper can also be used in place of green tomatoes in this recipe; just skip the mint and finish with some unpitted black olives. (I like to use unpitted olives, in the Italian way, but you can use pitted if you prefer.)

Refrigerated, the tomatoes will keep for a week; longer, if they're totally covered with oil.

> 2½ lb (1.2 kg) green tomatoes, no bigger than tennis balls, cored
> 2 tbsp kosher salt, divided
> 6 large cloves garlic, peeled, and sliced
> 1¼ cup (300 ml) olive oil
> 3 cups (720 ml) white, white wine, or apple cider vinegar
> 3 cups (720 ml) water
> 1 tbsp sugar
> 6 sprigs mint, picked, larger leaves torn
> 1 tsp chili pepper flakes

Use a sharp knife to cut the tomatoes into ¼-inch (.5-cm) rounds. It is very important that the slices are the same thickness, so that they will cook evenly. Sprinkle them on both sides with 1 tablespoon of the salt and allow them to drain in a colander.

Slice the garlic very thinly (I use a mandoline). In a saucepan, over a very, very low flame or pilot light, "bloom" the garlic slices in the olive oil. (Blooming is gently warming the garlic—barely cooking it—just to take the raw edge off the taste. It provides for a warm, softer flavor without the bite of raw garlic.)

Combine the vinegar, water, second tablespoon of salt, and sugar in a medium, nonreactive saucepan and bring the poaching liquid to a simmer. Taste the liquid. It should be salty, sweet, and sour—balanced and bright, not too strong or overpowering. All vinegars are different, so the brine may need adjustment. Because the tomatoes do not have the usual time to mellow in their brine, it should be more like a salad dressing than a pickle liquid. (Since the green tomatoes already have a sourness of their own, if they are cooked in a solution that is too vinegary and sour, they will not be pleasant to eat.)

In several batches, simmer the tomatoes in the brine for about 4 minutes. The tomatoes should be almost cooked through but still have a pleasant crunch, much like a cucumber pickle. The tomatoes will continue to cook for another minute after they are taken out of the poaching liquid, so pull them from the pan sooner rather than later. Err on the side of caution; you can always re-boil an underdone tomato, but you can't save a mushy, overcooked one. If the tomato skin begins to fall off while boiling, you are overcooking them. They should still have their integrity and remain in round, firm slices.

Use a slotted spoon to remove the slices from the simmering brine and allow them to cool on a sheet pan in a single layer. When cool, taste for salt, adding more if needed.

In a large ceramic dish, casserole, or jar, layer the tomatoes with the garlic-studded oil, torn mint, and chili pepper. For best results, allow to rest in the refrigerator overnight. If the tomatoes are not fully submerged in the oil, make sure to flip them over a few times while they marinate.

FAGIOLI ALL'UCCELLETTO
BEANS IN THE STYLE OF LITTLE BIRDS

Serves 4

A fall favorite at RSFP, this dish is also served at the Academy favorite pizzeria Ai Marmi. The recipe is Tuscan in origin; in fact, Tuscans are often called mangiafagioli, *"bean eaters." With the addition of rendered pork sausage, this can be served as a heavier side dish, or as an entree. The* all'uccelletto *of the recipe's name refers to sage and garlic, which are often used to flavor roasted game birds.*

> 1 lb (454 g) dried white beans, soaked overnight (use fresh
>   beans when in season)
> Aromatics in any combination: bay leaf, sprigs of sage and
>   rosemary, carrot, celery, peeled garlic and onion
> ½ cup (120 ml) olive oil, plus additional for the tomato
> Kosher salt
> 4 cloves garlic, peeled and smashed
> A pinch of chili pepper flakes
> 1 large bunch sage, picked, larger leaves torn in half
> 1 (28 oz / 794 g) can whole San Marzano—style tomatoes,
>   crushed by hand into small chunks

When you are ready to cook, rinse and drain the beans, put them in a pot and cover with fresh water. Bring to a boil, then reduce to a bare simmer, skimming any foam that rises to the top. Once the foam is removed, add in the aromatics, along with ½ cup (120 ml) olive oil. Once the beans are cooked, season with salt, and allow them to rest in their liquid for at least a few hours; overnight is better.

In a wide pan large enough to hold all the beans, heat enough olive oil to cover the bottom of the pan. Add in the smashed garlic and cook slowly with little browning. Add the chili pepper and sage and, still over low heat, cook them gently to infuse the oil with their flavors.

Carefully tip the tomato into the pan and simmer until the oil and tomato are combined. Drain the beans, reserving the liquid, and add them to the pan. Add the bean liquid back into the pan as needed to keep the beans barely submerged. Simmer for 10 to 15 minutes to allow the sauce to combine, being careful not to overcook the beans. Add additional salt if needed.

FAGIOLI CON LE COTICHE

BEANS WITH PORK SKIN

Serves 4

Pork skin is a byproduct of butchering that is often thrown away, but in this recipe, with its origins in the cucina povera, it is used to add flavor and complexity. Just down the hill from the Academy, in Testaccio, the pizzeria De Remo serves a famous version of this dish.

> 1 lb (454 g) dried white beans, soaked overnight (use fresh beans when in season)
>
> Aromatics in any combination: bay leaf, sprigs of sage and rosemary, carrots, celery, garlic, peeled onion
>
> ½ cup (120 ml) olive oil, plus additional for the soffritto
>
> 2 lb (907 g) fresh pork skin, all fat, hair, and blemishes removed, cut into ½-inch strips
>
> Kosher salt
>
> 1 carrot, peeled and diced
>
> 1 stalk celery, diced
>
> 1 small onion, peeled and diced
>
> 2 cloves garlic, peeled and smashed
>
> A pinch of chili pepper flakes
>
> 1 (28 oz / 794 g) can tomato puree
>
> ½ bunch parsley, picked and chopped

When you are ready to cook, rinse and drain the beans, put them in a pot, and cover with fresh water. Bring to a boil then reduce to a bare simmer, skimming any foam that rises to the top. Once the foam is removed, add in the aromatics, along with ½ cup (120 ml) olive oil. Once the beans are cooked, season with salt and allow them to rest in their liquid for at least a few hours; overnight is better.

While the beans are cooking, prepare the skin. Boil the strips of pork skin in lightly salted water, until they can be easily pierced with a fork, about 1½ to 2 hours. When tender, remove the skin and allow it to cool. Discard liquid. Use a knife to remove any cooked fat from the skin, and dice it into small, 1-inch (2-cm) rectangles.

In a wide saucepan over medium heat, make the *soffritto*: Add enough olive oil to coat the bottom of the pan, then add the carrot, celery, onion, and garlic. Slowly sweat the vegetables until soft and translucent. Stir in the tomato, add chili pepper and salt to taste, and bring to a simmer. Add in the cooked pork skin and simmer for about 10 minutes. Drain the beans, reserving their liquid, and add them to the pot. Add the bean liquid back into the pan as needed to keep the beans barely submerged, and slowly cook for 10 to 15 minutes more until the mixture is creamy and emulsified. Add additional salt if needed, fold in the parsley, and serve.

CICERCHIE IN UMIDO

GRASS PEAS STEWED WITH CARROT, CELERY & ONION

Serves 4 to 6

Sometimes translated as "chicklings" or "pulses," cicerchie were cultivated in Mesopotamia as early as 8000 BC. This ancient legume is now recognized officially by the Italian Ministry of Forestry and Agriculture as "a product of Italy's traditional agriculture."

These peas contain a toxin that can be dangerous if eaten in quantity for a prolonged period. Though we don't serve enough of them to be remotely dangerous, in order to remove the toxins, we soak cicerchie in abundant water overnight, then blanch them three times before cooking them slowly, like other beans. The triple blanching is unnecessary if you're using chickpeas.

This dish is a perfect match for the Roasted Pork Shoulder (page 53).

> 1 lb (454 g) dried cicerchie or chickpeas, soaked for 12 to
>   24 hours, in advance, and, if using cicerchie, simmered
>   and drained three times as described below
> Kosher salt
> Olive oil
> 1 large carrot, peeled and cut into small dice
> 1 red onion, peeled and cut into small dice
> 1 stalk celery, peeled and cut into small dice
> 3 stalks rosemary, picked and roughly chopped
> 3 cloves garlic, peeled and smashed
> 2 fresh bay leaves
> A large pinch of chili pepper flakes
> 1 tbsp tomato paste or 1 cup (225 g) tomato puree

When you are ready to cook, if you are using *cicerchie*, rinse and drain the peas, put them in a pot and cover with fresh water. Bring the peas to a simmer, then drain. Repeat this "simmer and drain" process again, and a third time, bring the peas to a boil, then reduce to a simmer and cook until tender, about 1 hour. Skim any foam that rises to the top. Season with salt and let the peas cool in their liquid at room temperature. If you are using chickpeas, follow the directions above but omit the "simmer and drain" process.

While the peas rest in their liquid, start the *soffritto*. In a pot large enough to eventually fit all of the peas, warm up enough olive oil over medium heat to cover the bottom of the pan. Add the vegetables, garlic, herbs, and chili pepper and sweat until the mixture starts to soften. Season with a pinch of salt. Add the tomato and fry until it turns a dark rusty color.

Once the tomato darkens, drain the peas, reserving the liquid, and stir them into the pot. Add about 2 cups (480 ml) of the pea cooking liquid to the pot until the mixture is well hydrated. Cook for about 20 minutes, until the flavors come together and the mixture starts to get slightly creamy.

Check for seasoning—the peas might need more salt or chili pepper—and then finish with a big glug of good olive oil. Even better, if you're serving this with Roasted Pork Shoulder, stir in any drippings from the roasted meat. Stir well to emulsify the fat and serve.

PATATE AL FORNO
ROASTED POTATOES

Serves 4 to 6

I have been told by many interns that this is the one recipe they will always carry with them. More of a technique than a recipe, it is a simple procedure that will forever change the way you cook potatoes. Impregnating the outside of the cooked potato with the herby oil results in an exterior that is very crispy and an interior with the consistency of mashed potatoes. Our lovely dipendenti, *or workers, are truly a meat-and-potatoes crowd; they love this dish, especially when the potatoes are the dry-farmed variety from our farmer Giovanni Bernabei.*

> Kosher salt
> 2 lb (.900 g) roasting potatoes, scrubbed, peeled or left
>   unpeeled, and cut into 2-inch (5-cm) chunks or wedges
> ¾ cup (180 ml) olive oil
> 4 cloves garlic, unpeeled
> 2 sprigs rosemary, picked
> 2 sprigs sage, picked

Preheat the oven to 400°F (205°C).

Bring a large pot of water to a boil. Season the water with salt (make it salty, as if you were cooking pasta). Boil the potatoes for about 6 to 8 minutes until the outer edges of the potato have a "fuzzy" look, but the potato is not quite cooked all the way through.

While the potatoes boil, add the oil, garlic, and herbs to a large metal bowl. When the potatoes are ready, drain them, and put the hot potatoes into the bowl. Using a large spoon, vigorously move everything around so the potatoes are coated with the oil, herbs, and garlic.

Slide the potatoes, along with all the oil and herbs, onto a roasting tray. (Do not use parchment paper, which discourages browning.)

Roast for about 1 hour and 20 minutes, turning the potatoes over every 20 minutes. If the potatoes look dry, do not hesitate to add more olive oil. Remember: FAT = FLAVOR.

INSALATA DI PUNTARELLE
CON ACCIUGHE, PEPE NERO E MOZZARELLA
PUNTARELLE SALAD WITH ANCHOVY,
BLACK PEPPER & MOZZARELLA

Serves 4 to 6

This is a quintessential Roman salad, made from the bitter green curls of Catalonian chicory, dressed with garlic, anchovy, lemon juice and/or vinegar, black pepper, and olive oil. It is not a subtle salad; its flavors are strong and bracing. The bright flavors of this salad are the perfect foil for a fatty meat course.

In my recipe, I like to up the ante by using whole fillets of anchovy in addition to the ones that are made into a paste and stirred into the dressing. I also like to add hand-torn strips of fresh mozzarella. The combination of fish, cheese, and the acidic dressing may seem odd at first, but all of the flavors and textures combine deliciously. Romans are stoic about their food rules, but the one they often bend is the precept against combining fish and cheese. A good example of that is the Roman classic, mozzarella in carozza, a grilled cheese sandwich served with anchovy sauce.

I make the dressing immediately before serving. If it is made too far in advance, the vinegar really "cooks" the anchovy and makes for a muddy flavor. The flavors should be sharp and assertive.

If you cannot find puntarelle, you can substitute sliced young dandelion greens, sliced endive, shaved fennel, or any combination of those. Remember, for this dish, BITTER = BETTER.

> ½ lb (227 g) puntarelle or other bitter greens
> 1 clove garlic, peeled
> 6 anchovy fillets, divided
> Kosher salt
> 3 tbsp white wine vinegar and/or lemon juice
> ½ cup (120 ml) extra virgin olive oil
> ½ lb (227 g) fresh mozzarella
> Coarsely ground black pepper

Prepare the *puntarelle* by pulling away the thin green outer leaves. Reserve them for cooking another time. You should be left with the hollow, center heart of *puntarelle*. Pull away each stalk, and use a paring knife to trim away the woody bottom from each piece. If you have a *puntarelle* cutter, shred each stalk through the screen.

Without a cutter, simply slice the *puntarelle* into small matchsticks, discarding any hard, woody pieces.

Let the prepared *puntarelle* sit in ice water for at least 1 hour while you prepare the dressing. Sitting in the ice water allows the *puntarelle* to lose excess bitterness and curl up. If you are using dandelion green, endive, or fennel, it is not necessary to soak them in ice water.

For the dressing, use a mortar and pestle to make a paste out of the garlic and three of the anchovy fillets; add a small pinch of salt for abrasion. Add in the vinegar and/ or lemon juice (I like a combination), then the oil. As you use the mortar to emulsify the oil into the dressing, it will thicken. The vinaigrette needs to be pretty dense in order to stick to the very smooth *puntarelle* or greens.

Tear the mozzarella into strips with your hands.

Drain the greens and spin them in a salad spinner. (It is important to dry them completely or the dressing will be too watery.) Put them in a bowl and toss vigorously with the dressing to coat. Gently fold in the remaining anchovy filets and the torn mozzarella. Add some generous grinds of black pepper.

Adjust the acid and seasonings if necessary and serve immediately.

INSALATA DI CETRIOLI GRIGLIATI
GRILLED CUCUMBER SALAD

Serves 4

A take on the Greek condiment tzatziki, this lemony, herby, crunchy salad is great as a standalone, or served with a piece of grilled or roasted meat (we have served this with the Pork Tenderloin with Herb & Breadcrumb Crust (page 61) at the annual Cortile Dinner). We use these cucumbers as a salad, and we also use them to make a condiment or salsa.

> 3 large cucumbers, peeled (unpeeled if using hothouse cucumbers)
> Kosher salt
> ½ small white onion, peeled and minced
> Juice of 1 lemon
> 1 clove garlic, peeled and mashed to a paste
> 1 tbsp dill, finely chopped
> 1 tbsp parsley, finely chopped
> 1 tsp mint, finely chopped
> 1 cup (275 g) Greek or strained yogurt
> About ½ cup (120 ml) olive oil
> Coarsely ground black pepper

Heat a grill pan on the stovetop or charcoal grill outside to a very high temperature. Cut the cucumbers in half lengthwise. Pat dry with a paper towel, and grill the cucumbers flesh side down for about 5 minutes without moving. Cook until they are evenly blackened and then remove from the grill. They should still be mostly crunchy and uncooked. Season with salt and place them in the refrigerator to cool for about 15 minutes. Mix the minced onion and a pinch of salt into the lemon juice, and let macerate for at least 15 minutes.

To make the salad, slice the cucumbers at an angle into 2-inch (5-cm) pieces. Combine the remaining ingredients with the onions and lemon, then fold in the sliced cucumbers. Adjust the seasoning and serve immediately.

If you plan to use this as a condiment for meat, seed the grilled cucumbers and dice them into small pieces. Combine with the dressing as above and serve.

MISTICANZA

MIXED FORAGED GREENS

Serves 4 to 6

Misticanza alla Romana is a classic combination of young, tender, wild greens that are simply dressed with oil, salt, and vinegar or lemon. Romans have long been enamored of this mix of greens. Since it's fairly impossible to find all of these greens—it's even difficult in Rome!—the home cook can use a mixture of what's available. Balance is the important part; ideally, include a green that is peppery (such as arugula), bitter (radicchio), sweet and crunchy (cabbage), aromatic (fennel with its fronds), and fresh herbs and spicy chives. The salad should also be carefully dressed so that each green can shine. Misticanza is a great complement for fatty meats, and can be served as a starter, alongside the meat, or as a palate-cleansing finish to a meal.

> 1 small head curly endive, white/light green parts only, chopped
> into 2-inch (5-cm) pieces
> 1 small head escarole, white/light green parts only, chopped
> into 2-inch (5-cm) pieces
> 1 small head radicchio, chopped into 2-inch (5-cm) pieces
> White wine vinegar or lemon, or a combination
> Olive oil
> Kosher salt
> ½ bunch chives, chopped into 2-inch (5-cm) lengths
> Handful of mixed soft herb leaves, such as parsley, mint,
> tarragon, chervil, left whole

Carefully wash and dry all the greens. Resist the urge to cut them up too much; leave the smaller leaves as intact as possible.

In the bottom of a salad bowl, add a splash of vinegar and/or lemon juice (I like a combination), some olive oil, and a pinch of salt. Use your fingertips to stir vigorously to bring the dressing together. Taste and adjust. There is no recipe for this dressing because the greens will always be different, as will the oil and vinegar you use. Start with less dressing than you need; you can always add more to the bowl once the greens are in, but you can't fix the salad once it's overdressed.

Once the dressing is the right balance of salt, sour, and oil, add the greens, chives, and herbs to the bowl and, with your hands, drag them gently through the dressing. Taste and serve.

INSALATA DI RADICCHIO CON MELE VERDE, ACETO BALSAMICO E NOCI TOSTATE

RADICCHIO SALAD WITH GREEN APPLES, BALSAMIC VINEGAR & TOASTED WALNUTS

Serves 4 to 6

In the winter, bitter salad greens such as radicchio are abundant. This salad works because the bitter radicchio is balanced by the sweet and sour flavors of the balsamic vinegar and green apples. The whole parsley leaves are palette-cleansing, and the toasted nuts bring that salty crunch that keeps you coming back for more.

> ½ cup (60 g) walnut halves
> Olive oil
> Kosher salt
> 2 heads radicchio (I prefer the Treviso variety)
> 2 green apples, stems removed, divided
> ¼ cup (60 ml) balsamic vinegar
> 1 tbsp apple cider or white wine vinegar
> ½ cup (120 ml) mild olive oil, plus additional for toasting walnuts
> Honey

Preheat the oven to 300°F (150°C). Toast the walnuts for 10 to 12 minutes, stirring them every few minutes, until light golden brown. Allow them to cool, then break them with your hands or chop with a knife into pieces. Toss the pieces with a small amount of olive oil and salt and set aside.

Separate the radicchio leaves from the base of the plant, pulling away the whole leaves. Wash and dry them carefully, then tear the larger leaves into pieces.

Chop one of the apples, along with its skin and seeds, and puree it in a food processor with the vinegars. Strain the puree through a sieve, pressing down to release all the juice. Put the puree in a bowl and whisk in olive oil and honey to taste. There is no exact amount for the honey, because it will depend on how sweet the apples and balsamic vinegar are. Season with salt.

Slice the remaining apple into thin slices, discarding the core. Combine the radicchio, dressing, nuts, and sliced apples. You may not use all of the dressing. Adjust for seasoning and serve.

CRAUTI

SAUERKRAUT

Winter brings a huge harvest of cabbage from our farmers, so sauerkraut is the best way to use up the excess. The caraway and bay leaf is a base flavor; feel free to add more if you like. I keep the aromatics to a minimum so I have more options when using the sauerkraut in different dishes over the course of the winter and spring.

My favorite way to eat this (besides by itself!) is to rinse it and stew it down with cooked onions, apples, and apple juice, much like the recipe in the RSFP cookbook, Verdure.

> *Cabbage, shredded*
> *Kosher salt*
> *Caraway seed*
> *Bay leaves*

Weigh and shred the cabbage and add 2½% salt by weight. Add 1 gram of caraway seed and one fresh bay leaf per 2.2 lb (1 kg) of cabbage. In a bowl, massage the cabbage with the ingredients and allow it to macerate overnight, covered, in the refrigerator.

Transfer the cabbage to a crock or jar. Pack the cabbage down into the container and weigh it down with a zip-lock bag filled with salted water (salted, so if the bag breaks the kraut will not be ruined). Cover the container with a cloth, such as a dish towel, to keep bugs and dust out while allowing the carbon dioxide that is produced during fermentation to escape. Let the sauerkraut ferment until the right amount of sourness is achieved and the bubbling stops. The more sauerkraut you make, the longer it will take. A small batch will take about 2 weeks.

ZUCCA IN AGRODOLCE
SWEET AND SOUR SQUASH

Serves 4 to 6

The idea for this dish grew out of the Italian method of preservation called in scapece, *in which vegetables or fish are floured and fried, then submerged in a sweet and sour vinegar bath, often with onion and, in Sicilian recipes, raisins.*

> ½ cup (85 g) golden raisins
> 2 tbsp apple cider vinegar or white wine vinegar
> Kosher salt
> Sugar
> 1 tsp chili pepper flakes
> 2 small red onions
> Extra virgin olive oil
> 2 tbsp red wine vinegar
> 1 large butternut squash, peeled, halved, seeded,
>   and cut horizontally into ½-in (1-cm) strips

Preheat the oven to 350°F (175°C).

First, pickle the raisins. In a small pot, combine the raisins, apple cider or white wine vinegar, a pinch each of salt and sugar, chili pepper, and just enough water to cover. Simmer over low heat for 15 minutes, then remove from heat and allow the raisins to cool in the liquid. This can be done several days ahead.

Halve and peel the onions and cut each half into four or six wedges depending on size. (You want the wedges to stay intact and not separate.) In a bowl, sprinkle the onions with salt, olive oil, and the red wine vinegar and toss. Place them on a sheet pan that is lined with parchment paper. Use your fingertips to spritz some water onto the pan to help steam the onions and allow them to cook through without burning.

Toss the squash pieces in the same bowl with additional salt and oil. Spread them onto a different roasting tray, also lined with parchment paper. Put both trays in the oven and cook for about 25 minutes, sprinkling more water on the onions if necessary. The onions will be done first. Allow everything to cool to room temperature.

To compose the plate: shingle the squash pieces first, then top with the onions. Sprinkle with the pickled raisins, allowing some of the pickling liquid to dribble on top of the dish. If the plate looks a little dry, finish with a nice glug of olive oil.

INSALATA DI CARCIOFI CRUDI
RAW ARTICHOKE SALAD

———

Serves 4

Romans are obsessed with artichokes, and, lucky for them, Rome has two distinct artichoke seasons, fall and spring. The early season artichokes are super tender while the Roman variety comes later and has very little choke and a large central heart.

This is a fresh take on Carciofi alla romana, *artichokes stewed with lemon, parsley, and mint. This salad uses thinly sliced artichoke hearts, and they're served raw, but because they're heavily dressed with lemon, the artichoke is "cooked" by the acid and is bleached to a much lighter color. The lemon helps to tenderize and flavor this sturdy thistle.*

To serve as a stand-alone salad, I like to add arugula and Parmigiano Reggiano. If serving with a meat dish, like the Cotolette alla milanese *(page 57), I omit them.*

> 8 small artichokes, trimmed of all tough outer
>   leaves, stems peeled, sliced as thinly as possible
> Juice of 1 large lemon, plus additional if needed
> Kosher salt
> Olive oil
> Coarsely ground black pepper
> 6 sprigs parsley, picked, large leaves torn
> 6 sprigs mint, picked, large leaves torn
> 1 small bunch arugula, washed and dried (optional)
> Shavings of Parmigiano Reggiano (optional)

Macerate the sliced artichokes with the lemon juice and a few pinches of salt for at least 30 minutes before serving.

When ready to serve, move the artichokes to another bowl, leaving behind the lemon juice. To the lemon juice, add olive oil, pepper, parsley, and mint, and mix to incorporate. If the salad needs more acid, add some more lemon juice. If desired, serve over a bed of arugula, and/or topped with shavings of Parmigiano Reggiano.

INSALATA TRITATA

CHOPPED SALAD

———

Serves 4 to 6

Ross, our previous third cook, always joked that my Friday Family Night dinner menus, more often than not, leaned pretty heavily into New Jersey Italian-American territory (I'm from North Jersey). He called them my Sopranos menus. I've been know to lay on the accent on Fridays: "mutzadel," "manigot," "prushoot," etc.

This chopped salad has all the celebrated flavors of a good Jersey deli "antipasto": crunchy chopped vegetables, provolone, salami, and pickled peppers doused in a red-wine vinegar and oregano dressing. This one brings me back to my childhood.

Feel free to add hard-boiled egg, grated carrots, red onion, boiled potato, croutons, and more; the ingredients can be mixed and matched depending on what is in season, or what you have in your fridge.

Some chopped salads are cut so small you can eat them with a spoon! I prefer a chunkier chop.

> 1 small red bell pepper, cored, seeded, and cut into 1-inch
>   (2.5-cm) strips
> ½ cup (120 ml) red wine vinegar
> Kosher salt
> ¾ cup (180 ml) olive oil
> 1 tbsp Dijon mustard
> ½ clove garlic, peeled and mashed into a paste
> A large pinch of dried oregano
> A large pinch of coarsely ground black pepper
> ¼ lb (113g) sharp provolone or low-moisture mozzarella, diced
> ¼ lb (113g) salami, diced
> ½ cup (100 g) green olives with pimentos, chopped
> 1 fennel bulb, diced
> ½ pint cherry tomatoes, halved
> 6 radishes, thinly sliced
> 1 head Romaine lettuce, chopped
> 1 head round radicchio, chopped

Prepare the quick-pickled red pepper: Slice the pepper and dress it with the red wine vinegar and a pinch of salt. Use your fingertips to massage the salt and vinegar into the pepper and set aside for at least 20 minutes while you prepare the rest of the ingredients.

Make the dressing: Whisk together the olive oil, mustard, garlic, oregano, and pepper. Drain the red peppers and reserve them and add their vinegar to the dressing. The dressing should remain broken, not fully emulsified.

Mix the remaining salad ingredients in a large bowl, then stir the dressing and add to the bowl. Unlike the Misticanza salad, this should be dressed strongly. Jersey-strong.

TALLI DI AGLIO CON OLIVE E POMODORO
GARLIC SCAPES WITH OLIVES & TOMATO

Serves 4 to 6

One spring, one of our farmers, Antonella, starting sending us garlic scapes. At one point we were so buried in them that I reached out to my buddy, John Adler of Franny's in Brooklyn, to ask for suggestions. He passed this recipe on to me. It's just as delicious when made with green beans.

> 1 lb (454 g) garlic scapes or green beans, cut into 3-inch
>   (7.5-cm) pieces
> 1 cup (240 ml) olive oil, divided
> Kosher salt
> ½ cup (125 g) tomato paste
> 2 tsp fennel seeds
> A pinch of chili pepper flakes
> 1 tsp dried oregano or 2 tsp fresh oregano, chopped
> 1 cup (240 ml) white wine
> 1 cup (240 ml) water
> 1 cup (200 g) green olives, chopped
> ¼ cup (60 ml) red wine vinegar

Preheat the oven to 450°F (230°C).

Mix the garlic scapes with ½ cup of the olive oil and season with salt. Roast them on a tray until golden brown. Remove and hold at room temperature.

Lower the oven to 350°F (175°C).

In a saucepan over a medium flame, heat the remaining ½ cup of the olive oil, add the tomato paste and fry until it turns brick-red. Mix in the fennel seeds, chili pepper, and oregano and cook for 30 seconds. Immediately pour over the roasted scapes.

In a baking dish or sauté pan with a tight-fitting lid, combine the scapes and all of their oil with the white wine and water. Cover with parchment paper and then a lid or foil and bake at 350°F (175°C) for 1½ hours.

After 1½ hours, remove lid or foil and add in the chopped olives. Return the pan to the oven and bake for an additional 20 minutes. Remove from oven, mix with vinegar and allow to cool completely.

BASICS

SALSE PER BOLLITO
SAUCES FOR BOLLITO

Because the meat is simply boiled with wine and few aromatics, bollito *lacks the added flavor of caramelization provided by grilling or searing. The real stars of the boiled dinner are the sauces—their spicy, sour, and sweet flavors are perfect foils for the fatty, gelatinous meat. Of the dozens of sauces served with* bollito, *these are my eight favorites.*

SALSA VERDE · GREEN SAUCE

This is the classic Roman green sauce. Sometimes I make my own interpretation, which includes quick-pickled minced red onion.

> ½ cup (75 g) salt-packed capers, purged of salt (see below)
>   and chopped
> 1 clove of garlic, peeled and minced to a paste
> ½ bunch parsley, picked and chopped
> Juice of 1 lemon
> 1 cup (240 ml) olive oil
> Kosher salt, if needed

Purge the capers by rinsing off the excess salt, then simmer them in water for about 2 minutes. (Do not boil.) Drain, add fresh water, and simmer the capers for another 2 minutes. Drain and set aside.

Combine the capers and garlic. Mix in the parsley, then stir in the lemon juice and about a cup of good olive oil. Taste and season with salt if needed.

SALSA RUSTICA · GREEN SAUCE WITH BREADCRUMBS & EGG

> 1 cup (40 g) country bread, torn into pea-sized pieces
> Red wine vinegar
> 2 eggs, hard-boiled and finely chopped

Make Salsa Verde, omitting the lemon juice. Soak the bread in red wine vinegar for about 15 minutes. Squeeze out the bread and add it to the Salsa Verde. Finely chop the eggs and fold them into the mixture. Stir to combine.

SALSA ROSSA · RED SAUCE

Italian ketchup!

> 1 small onion, peeled and diced
> ½ carrot, peeled and diced
> ½ red bell pepper, cored, seeded, and diced
> 2 cloves of garlic, peeled and smashed
> ½ cup (120 ml) olive oil
> A pinch of kosher salt, plus additional if needed
> A pinch of chili pepper flakes, plus additional if needed
> ½ cup red wine vinegar, plus additional if needed
> 1 tbsp honey
> 5 or 6 tomatoes (fresh in season, or canned), peeled, seeded, and diced
> A handful of basil leaves

In a small saucepan, sauté the onion, carrot, bell pepper, and garlic in olive oil until soft. Add a pinch of salt and chili pepper, then the red wine vinegar and honey. Add the diced tomatoes and cook until thick and fragrant. Add the basil and puree. Cool to room temperature, taste, and add more salt, chili pepper, or vinegar, if needed.

SENAPE · MUSTARD

Mustard has Roman origins. The word is derived from the Latin mustum ardens, *which means "burning must"—in Roman times mustard was prepared with unfermented grape juice, or must. Prepared mustard is featured in the first written cookbook, by Apicius, which dates from the first century.*

> ½ cup (70 g) mustard seeds (black or yellow)
> ½ cup (70 g) mustard powder
> ½ cup (120 ml) red or white wine or cider vinegar
> ½ cup (120 ml) water
> Kosher salt

Combine the mustard seeds with the mustard powder, vinegar, water, and a few pinches of salt. Allow to rest covered in the refrigerator for at least 24 hours before using.

MAIONESE · MAYONNAISE

When I serve Bollito Misto at room temperature, I like to serve it with mayonnaise; it's perfect for warmer weather.

> The yolk of 1 large egg
> 1 teaspoon Dijon mustard
> 1 cup (240 ml) mild
> vegetable oil
> Juice of 1 lemon
> Kosher salt

Put the yolk in a bowl; add the mustard and a splash of water. Whisk to combine, then slowly stream in the vegetable oil. Stir in the lemon juice and salt to taste.

CREN · HORSERADISH SAUCE

This sauce from northeastern Italy is super-dense and delicious.

> 2 eggs, hard-boiled
> 1 small horseradish root
> Sugar
> Kosher salt
> Freshly torn white breadcrumbs soaked in white wine vinegar
> Heavy cream

Peel the eggs, remove the cooked yolks and mash them with a fork (reserve the whites for another use). Peel and very finely grate the horseradish root. In a bowl, combine the egg yolks, the horseradish, a few pinches of sugar and salt. Lightly squeeze the vinegar-soaked breadcrumbs to remove excess vinegar, then stir into the mixture, along with some heavy cream, until the consistency of the Cren is that of a thick paste.

MOSTARDA DI FRUTTA · FRUIT & MUSTARD SAUCE

Mostarda di Frutta is a condiment of whole candied fruits preserved in syrup spiked with sharp mustard oil. It's hard to find in the U.S., and although it's widely available in Italy, we make our own. In commercial mostardas, the essential oil of mustard is used, which has the advantages of transparency and strength; in home cooking, mustard powder heated in white wine may be used, but it does not provide that wasabi-like bite. In our kitchen, we reproduce the potency of the mustard oil by using ground yellow mustard powder. What fruit we add depends on the season; in summer, we like to use apricots or plums from our garden, when they are still very green. The result is sweet, sour, and spicy! Ripe fruit, or a combination of ripe and unripe, works equally well; ripe fruit provides sweetness, unripe fruit brings sourness. And you can use fruits other than stone fruits.

Refrigerated, the mostarda will keep for one week.

> ½ cup (70 g) yellow mustard seeds
> White wine vinegar
> A pinch of kosher salt
> A pinch of sugar
> ½ cup (70 g) mustard powder
> About 1 cup (175 g) green stone fruit, such as apricots or plums, diced

Pickle the mustard seeds in a solution of two parts white wine vinegar to one part water, along with a heavy pinch of both salt and sugar by boiling for 30 minutes and then allowing them to plump overnight in the solution. The next day, drain the pickled seeds (reserving the pickling solution) and combine them with the mustard powder, some of the reserved liquid, and the fruit.

PEARÀ · VENETIAN BREAD SAUCE

Pearà means "peppered" in the Venetian dialect. The sauce should be thick, creamy, and peppery.

> Butter or extra virgin olive oil
> Beef bone marrow
> Fine, dry breadcrumbs
> Beef broth
> Coarsely ground black pepper
> Parmigiano
> Kosher salt

To make: Take equal parts butter (or olive oil) and beef bone marrow and melt them in a heavy bottomed pot. Sprinkle in fine, dry breadcrumbs until the fat is absorbed. Then ladle in an amount of boiling hot broth equivalent to twice the volume of the breadcrumb mix. Cook over low heat for at least 2 hours and finish with a generous amount of freshly ground black pepper and finely grated Parmigiano. Salt to taste.

POLENTA

Serves 6 to 8

Never use pre-cooked, quick-cook, or bargain brands of polenta. If the only polenta you have is of less-than-great quality, use meat broth instead of water to bolster the flavor, and finish with lots of butter and cheese.

In this recipe, I use a 5:1 ratio of water to polenta, which results in loose polenta. If you want stiff polenta for grilling, you can use a 4:1 ratio. If the polenta is of exceptional quality, I often skip the butter at the end of cooking so that the bright corn flavor can shine.

I am not a purist who insists polenta must be stirred clockwise, constantly. Polenta is not risotto, and the stirring does not ensure smoothness; rather, the correct ratio of liquid, and how gently and evenly you stream the polenta into the water at the beginning, determines whether there are lumps or not.

You can reduce the cooking time by at least 30 minutes if you pre-soak the polenta for about 2 hours. If you pre-soak the polenta, you don't even have to boil the water first, just "throw everybody in the pool" and turn on the fire.

> *10 cups (about 2.5 l) water*
> *2 teaspoons kosher salt, plus additional for seasoning*
> *2 cups (340 g) medium or coarse grain polenta or cornmeal*
> *3 tablespoons butter*
> *Bring the water to a boil over high heat. Add the salt.*

Slowly stream the polenta into the water, whisking constantly to prevent clumps. Turn the heat down to low. Keep whisking for 3 to 5 minutes until the polenta thickens and you can no longer whisk easily.

When the polenta thickens up, switch to a sturdy wooden spoon. Continue cooking and stirring, about once every 10 minutes, until the polenta is done. It should take about one hour, depending on the brand and grind of the cornmeal. Make sure to move all of the polenta around the bottom of the pan as you stir.

If the polenta dries out too much during cooking, don't be afraid to add small amounts of water as you stir. (The grains of polenta need to stay hydrated in order to cook evenly.)

If the polenta starts to stick, do not try to scrape up the browned bottom, simply allow a crust to form and keep the heat low—if you are lucky you can peel the *crosta* away from the bottom of the pan when you are done. The crispy polenta crust is a delicious snack for the cook.

The best way to know when polenta is done is by tasting it for flavor—uncooked polenta is gritty and bitter, but fully cooked polenta is smooth and corn-sweet. The consistency should be runny and pourable. If not, add water in small increments while stirring over a medium flame until the right consistency is reached. Always re-check seasoning after adding water; if you water down the polenta, you will need to add more salt.

When the polenta is fully cooked, add the butter, stir until it melts, and serve.

SALSA GRAVY OR IL GRAVY

GRAVY

¼ cup solidified turkey fat from the turkey leg braise (or butter)
½ small white onion, peeled and minced
Turkey giblets (liver, heart, gizzard), cleaned and minced
2 tbsp fresh herbs, minced (thyme, parsley, sage)
¼ cup (32 g) all-purpose flour
2 cups (480 ml) turkey broth, hot (from the braised legs)
Kosher salt
A squeeze of lemon juice, if needed

Melt the turkey fat or butter in a small saucepan. Add in the onion, giblets, and herbs and gently sweat until the onions are tender and sweet, about 10 minutes.

Evenly sprinkle the flour over the onion mixture, making sure not to let the flour fall into clumps. Cook for a few minutes.

Whisk in the hot broth, making sure to break up any clumps of flour. Bring the gravy to a boil, then turn down to a low simmer. Cook for 5 to 10 minutes until the raw flour flavor dissipates, using a rubber spatula to scrape the bottom of the pan.

Season with salt and serve immediately. If the gravy tastes dull, a small squeeze of lemon juice right before serving will make the sauce brighter.

SALE AROMATIZZATO CON SALVIA
SAGE SALT

————

This technique of blending fresh herbs in salt can be done with pretty much any herb. By blending the herbs with salt, you ensure the herb flavor penetrates every part of the sausage. You can also use the flavored salts to season vegetables and any variety of other meats.

2 tsp kosher salt
1 tsp chopped fresh sage

Blend salt and sage in spice grinder or with a mortar and pestle until homogenous.

SPEZIE PER PÂTÉ
PÂTÉ SPICES

————

As with all spices, it's preferable to buy spices whole and grind them as you need them. Don't use old spices that have sat in the cupboard for decades!

1 tsp ground cloves
1 tsp ground nutmeg
1 tsp ground ginger
1 tsp ground coriander
1 tsp ground cinnamon
1 tsp ground white pepper

Combine all ingredients.

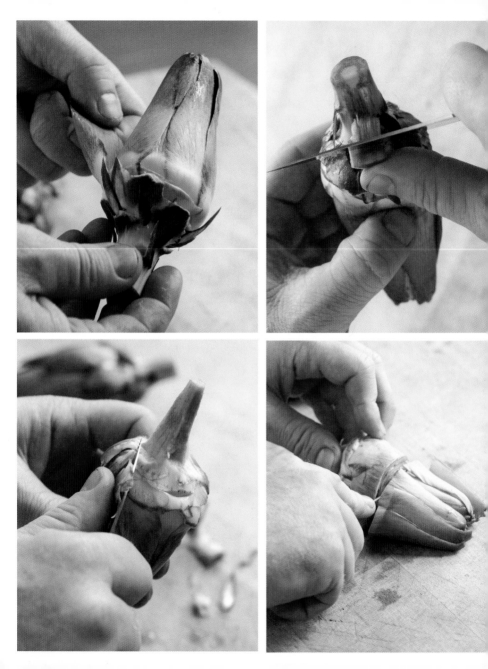

CLEANING ARTICHOKES

Artichokes are labor-intensive to clean—and the yield is small—yet their mesmerizing taste is a reward that makes the effort well worth it. Here in Rome we like to use globe artichokes because they have few or no thorns and they consistently have a more intense flavor than other varietals.

Prepare a large bowl with 1 gallon (3.8 l) of water and squeeze the juice of 1 lemon directly in the bowl; add the lemon halves as well. The acidity of the lemon juice prevents the artichokes from oxidizing and turning dark brown. Handle artichokes as quickly as possible, as they oxidize and turn brown as soon as they are peeled. Snap off the tough outer petals one at a time until you reach the pale colored petals of the heart of the artichoke. Using a small knife, pare away the dark green layer from the stem and around the base of the artichoke (there is a paler green layer underneath). Dip the artichoke in the lemon water and return it to the cutting board. Cut off the top of the artichoke flower to about 1 inch (2.5 cm) above the base. Immediately put the artichoke in the lemon water. Artichokes will keep for up to 24 hours submerged in lemon water.

If you need to slice the artichokes, remove the artichoke from the water and cut it in half lengthwise. Scoop out the choke (fuzzy part of the heart) using a small spoon. Dip the artichoke in the lemon water once again and return it to the board. Slice it according to the recipe you are using and keep in the lemon water until needed.

STABILIMENTO DI MATTAZIONE

RECIPE INDEX

A

Artichoke Salad, Raw 165
Insalata di carciofi crudi

B

Beans in the Style of
  Little Birds 145
Fagioli all'uccelletto

Beans with Pork Skin 146
Fagioli con le cotiche

Beef Stew 31
Spezzatino di manzo

Beef, Boiled 23
Bollito di manzo

Beef, Roast 21
Rosbeef

C

Chicken Saltimbocca 87
Saltimbocca di pollo

Chicken, Devil's-Style 89
Pollo alla diavola

Chicken, Roman-Style,
  Stewed with Tomatoes
  & Bell Peppers 83
Pollo alla Romana

Chicken, Stewed, with
  Vegetables 81
Stufato di pollo con verdure

Cucumber Salad, Grilled 155
Insalata di cetrioli grigliati

G

Garlic Scapes with Olives
  & Tomato 169
*Talli di aglio con olive
  e pomodoro*

Gravy 179
Salsa gravy or il gravy

Greens, Mixed Foraged 157
Misticanza

H

Ham, Cooked 113
Prosciutto cotto

L

Lamb Chops, Grilled with
  Roasted Shoulder 76
Abbacchio allo scottadito

Lamb Meatballs 127
Polpettine di agnello

Lamb, Baby, Braised in Egg,
  Lemon & Herb Sauce 72
Abbacchio brodettato

Lamb, Baby, Roasted,
  Roman-Style 69
Abbacchio alla romana

Liverwurst 129
Leberwurst

M

Mayonnaise 174
Maionese

Meatloaf, Stuffed 121
Polpettone ripieno

Mustard 173
Senape

P

Peas, Grass, Stewed with
   Carrot, Celery & Onion 148
Cicerchie in umido

Polenta 176
Polenta

Polenta with Pork Spare Ribs
   & Sausages 47
*Polenta con spuntature
   e salsicce*

Pork Belly, Quick-Cured 117
Pancetta fresca

Pork Chops, Breaded & Fried 57
Cotolette alla milanese

Pork Jowl, Cured 119
Guanciale

Pork Tenderloin with Herb
   & Breadcrumb Crust 61
*Filetto di maiale in crosta
   di erbe aromatiche*

Pork with "Tuna" Mayonnaise 50
Maiale "tonnato"

Pork, Mona's Milk-Braised 63
Maiale al latte di mona

Pork, Potted 134
Conserva di maiale

Pork, Roasted Shoulder 53
Spalla di maiale arrosto

Pork, Roasted with Herbs
   & Garlic 40
Porchetta

Pot Roast 35
Brasato di Manzo

Potatoes, Roasted 151
Patate al forno

Q

Quail, Oven-Roasted 93
Quaglie al forno

R

Rabbit Hunter's-Style 104
Coniglio alla cacciatora

Rabbit, Fried, Tuscan-Style 107
Coniglio fritto alla toscana

Rabbit, Grilled, with
   Olive Salsa 103
*Coniglio alla griglia con
salsa di olive*

Radicchio Salad with Green
   Apples, Balsamic Vinegar
   & Toasted Walnuts 159
*Insalata di radicchio con
   mele verde, aceto balsamico
   e noci tostate*

S

Sage Salt 181
Sale aromatizzato con salvia

Salad, Chopped 167
Insalata tritata

Salad, Cucumber, Grilled 155
Insalata di cetrioli grigliati

Salad, Puntarelle with Anchovy,
Black Pepper & Mozzarella 152
Insalata di puntarelle con acciughe,
  pepe nero e mozzarella

Salad, Radicchio with Green
  Apples, Balsamic Vinegar
  & Toasted Walnuts 159
Insalata di radicchio con
  mele verde, aceto balsamico
  e noci tostate

Salad, Raw Artichoke 165
Insalata di carciofi crudi

Sauce, Fruit & Mustard 174
Mostarda di frutta

Sauce, Green 172
Salsa verde

Sauce, Green with
  Breadcrumbs & Egg 172
Salsa rustica

Sauce, Horseradish 174
Cren

Sauce, Red 173
Salsa rossa

Sauce, Venetian Bread 175
Pearà

Sauces for Bollito 172
Salse per bollito

Sauerkraut 161
Crauti

Sausage, Pork 125
Salsiccia di maiale

Spices, Pâté 187
Spezie per pâté

Spread, Poultry Liver 137
Pâté di fegatini

Squash, Sweet and Sour 163
Zucca in agrodolce

Stew, Beef 31
Spezzatino di manzo

T

Terrine, Country 131
Terrina di campagna

Tomatoes, Pickled Green 143
Pomodori verdi sott'aceto

Turkey, Stuffed, for
  Thanksgiving 96
Tacchino ripieno del giorno
  del ringraziamento

V

Veal Marsala 28
Scaloppine al marsala

Veal Piccata 25
Piccata di vitello al limone

THE ROME SUSTAINABLE
FOOD PROJECT

Until 2007, a fellowship at the American Academy in Rome—arguably, the most prestigious prize awarded to archaeologists, painters, architects, scholars, and artists—had one huge drawback: the food. When the AAR's then-President, Adele Chatfield-Taylor, asked Alice Waters for help, Waters famously responded, "That depends. What do you want, better food or a revolution?" Without hesitation, Chatfield-Taylor replied, "A revolution." And a revolution—the Rome Sustainable Food Project—was ignited. Today, the collaboration of chefs, cooks, and interns, with the gardeners, artisan producers, and organic farmers who provide the raw ingredients results in the sixteen meals served each week to the artists and scholars in residence.

AMERICAN ACADEMY IN ROME

The American Academy in Rome is a center for independent study and advanced research in the arts and humanities. For more than 116 years the Academy has offered support, time and an inspiring environment to some of America's most gifted artists and scholars. Each year, through a national juried competition, the Academy offers up to thirty Rome prize fellowships in architecture, literature, musical composition, visual arts, and in humanistic approaches to ancient studies, medieval studies, Renaissance and early modern studies, and modern Italian studies. Fellows are joined by a select group of Residents, distinguished artists and scholars invited by the Director. Many Academy Fellows and Residents have had a significant influence in the world of art, music, culture, literature, scholarship and education.

Founded in 1894, the Academy was charted as a private institution by an act of Congress in 1905. The Academy remains a private institution supported by gifts from individuals, foundations and corporations, and the membership of colleges, universities and arts and cultural organizations, as well as by grants from the National Endowment for the Humanities and the United States Department of Education.

www.aarome.org

A NOTE ON THE TITLING TYPE

The Italian recipe titles are set in Saturn, a typeface based on the inscription on the Temple of Saturn in the Roman Forum. The word CARNE on the cover and title page was inspired by the butcher signs of Rome. Both were designed by Russell Maret, a letterpress printer & type designer who was the Rolland Rome Prize Fellow in Design at the American Academy in Rome in 2010.

ABCDEFGHIJKLMNOPQRSTUVWXYZ

ABOUT THE AUTHOR

In college, while majoring in English Lit, Chris Behr saw a "cook wanted" sign posted at his favorite bar. He offered to work for beer money, and without any formal training, ended up running the kitchen for the next two years, often skipping classes because he'd rather be cooking. He then went to culinary school, and was eventually hired to cook at the esteemed A16 in San Francisco, a restaurant pioneering Southern Italian farm-to-table cooking. He next was named *chef de cuisine* at SPQR, and in that capacity was sent twice to Rome to study the food there. After working in New York City at Balthazar Bakery and at Pulino's, he went on to BKLYN Larder where he propitiously met Mona Talbott, who eventually proposed him as sous chef for the Rome Sustainable Food Project. In 2014, he became the program's Executive Chef.

ABOUT THE PHOTOGRAPHER

Annie Schlechter has been working as a photographer since 1998. She spent from September 2009 to June 2010 living at the American Academy in Rome. Her clients include *New York Magazine, Veranda, Country Living, Condé Nast Traveler, Better Homes & Gardens, Coastal Living, House Beautiful, Travel + Leisure,* and *The World of Interiors.*

ACKNOWLEDGEMENTS

Above all, I want to thank my family for being so supportive. With just a few weeks notice, I up and moved to Rome, and they have been nothing but caring and encouraging on this long, strange trip. This book is dedicated to my mother, who is the best cook I know. After watching my mother put out restaurant-quality meals daily, wasting nothing, using vegetables from her own garden, for more than 30 years, it shouldn't surprise anyone that I've become the chef of a sustainable food program. Thanks, Mom.

Big thanks to Adele Chatfield-Taylor, former President of the American Academy in Rome; Mark Robbins, AAR President and CEO; Kim Bowes, AAR Director; the AAR Trustees; and the entire American Academy staff for their encouragement during this crazy book writing process. Shout out to all of the *dipendenti* of the American Academy, who have taught me more about Italian food and culture than anyone should ever know.

Thank you to all of the American Academy in Rome Fellows, Fellow Travelers, Residents, and Visiting Artists for being a part of our "Project." It is truly an honor to provide the fuel that feeds the fire of creativity and innovation at the Academy's dinner table.

The Little Bookroom for its continued support of the RSFP and our mission. These books are our legacy, and I could not be more proud or excited to be a part of this series. Immense and unending thanks to my editor/publisher/recipe-tester/cheerleader Angela Hederman. How many people have an editor who also tests all the recipes? I am lucky.

Annie Schlecter for the incredible photography. No one else can capture that Roman light quite like you, and I am beyond lucky to have your eyes behind that lens. It would be fair to say that you captured my true essence in my author photo: chicken wing eating bliss. To the woman who chased parking-lot chickens and stalked sheep for an entire afternoon: thank you.

Russell Maret for his truly masterful skill in designing the fonts for all of the RSFP cookbooks. Early on in the process for CARNE, he told me that the font for this book felt very "Via Marmorata," the road that parallels the huge, decommissioned slaughterhouse that is the heart of the nearby Testaccio district, and my favorite neighborhood. To say it was a perfect match would be an understatement. And thank you for being the voice of reason, forcing our photo-taking expedition in Sabina to make a pit stop for *porchetta* sandwiches.

Laura Offeddu, for constantly surprising me with her dedication, organization, and drive to keep the RSFP charging into the future. Your support over these last four years has been indispensable; I literally could not have done it without you.

Domenico Cortese, the CAPO, my trusted ally and sous chef. I am honored to have manned these stoves with you, and I wish you the best of luck as you jump into the beautiful ordeal of opening your own restaurant. *In bocca al lupo*, my friend. The RSFP has been more than lucky to have you and I speak for our entire community, past and present, when I wish you and Sofie the best.

Thank you to the New England Culinary Institute, for starting me down this road to Rome. A lifetime of thanks to my chef mentors Nate Appleman and Liza Shaw. You two taught me everything, from roasting beets to cooking beans to deboning a pig, and my career is based on the foundation you cemented. The RSFP interns hear my voice, but they are listening to your words. Thank you for the lessons in perseverance and dedication. Thanks to everyone in my San Francisco restaurant family, you all are part of who and where I am today.

So much gratitude to Alice Waters, who believed in me, and who supported me, and my cooking, despite the fact that I had never cooked at Chez Panisse. The lessons you've taught me about restraint and focus over these past few years are invaluable. Thank you Alice.

To all of the RSFP staff, past and present: An enormous thanks to Mona Talbott, for offering me this job on that rainy evening in Gowanus almost five years ago; Thanks to Chris Boswell, who welcomed me to this program and this life and immediately taught me a few things about the Italian diet and ALL of the Roman curse words; To Gio Guerrera, who showed me the ropes when I had just arrived in Rome; To Ross Phillips and Sara Levi for being the backbone of our kitchen team—your impact will be felt on the RSFP for years and years to come; To Gabriel Soare, Alessandro Lima, Tiziana Del Grosso, Tewelde Weldekidan, and Tesfamichel Ghebrehawareit for being the service staff that you wait your entire career to work with.

To the 2015-2016 RSFP interns and staff: Massimo Tripoli, Lorenzo Tirelli, Nolin Deloison Baum, Sarah Featherby, Henderson Peternell, Caspar Giri, Ji Hye Kim, Elena Mundrak, Stephen Shami, Andrew Nordstrom, Kimble Hicks, Leah Galler, Tom Finlayson, Jeremy Whyte, McLane Ritzel, Clementine Hain Cole, and Valentina Nuzzo.

Grazie infinite to Katie Parla, my pizza partner in crime for the last two years. Your knowledge, talent, drive, and love of spaghetti have brought me places I never thought I would go. Thank you, from the bottom of my heart, for showing me your Rome.

To Tamar Adler, not only for her beautiful words that open this book, but for involving me in the cooking class for *An Everlasting Meal* that resulted in my exportation to Rome. And to her brother John who, in that moment of awe after I was offered my dream job, looked me right in the eye and said: "If someone offers you a job in Italy, you don't think, you go."